FESTIVE ALLSORTS

Ideas for celebrating
the Christian year

Nicola Currie

Illustrations by
Julie Baines

National Society/Church House Publishing
Church House, Great Smith Street, London, SW1P 3NZ

ISBN 0 7151 4856 7

First published in 1994 by The National Society and Church House Publishing

Photocopying

Acknowledgements

The author and publisher gratefully acknowledge permission to reproduce copyright material in this anthology. Every effort has been made to trace and contact copyright holders. If there are any inadvertent omissions we apologise to those concerned.

Particular thanks are due to the *Church Times* for permission to reproduce the Allsorts pages from the *Church Times* 1990-1994.

Allsorts has relied on activity suggestions from many diocesan children's advisers, Sunday school teachers, children's workers and parents around Britain. The author and publisher wish particularly to thank the following people for their contributions to the chapters indicated: Olive Albon (St Alban), Mary Binks (Palm Sunday), Gillian Calvert (Mary Magdalene, Holy Cross Day, St Andrew), Joan Chapman (St Benedict, St Swithin), Sarah Condry (St Stephen, George Herbert, Julian of Norwich, Hildegard of Bingen), Anne Faulkner (St Lucy, Epiphany, St George, Trinity (with Peter Faulkner)), St John the Baptist, St Michael and All Angels, St Luke), Win Fish (Christmas, Candlemas, St Joseph, St Boniface, the Blessed Virgin Mary, St Martin), Mike Gardner and Kate Gardner (St Philip and St James, St James the Great), Ivor Hughes (St Matthias), Dorothy Jamal (St Patrick), Pam Jones (St Chad, Lent, St Mark, St Augustine, St Hilda), Susan Milton (Easter), Diana Murrie (St Nicholas, St Cuthbert, St Peter, St Thomas, St Oswald, All Saints' Day), Peter Privett (Week of Prayer for Christian Unity), Mandy Roberts (Advent, Mothering Sunday, St Cecilia), Pat Robins (St Bartholomew), Judith Sadler (Bede, the Transfiguration, St Aidan), Jean Thomson (St Antony, St David, Pentecost, St Columba, St Francis).

Bible quotations are from the The Revised Standard Version (RSV), © The National Council of Churches of Christ in the USA.

Thanks are also due to Geoffrey Chapman and Mowbray for an extract from The Sayings of the Desert Fathers translated by Benedicta Ward SLG; Darton, Longman and Todd Ltd, for an extract from *In Search of Julian of Norwich* by Sheila Upjohn; The Ven. G.B. Timms for his collect on St David; Penguin Books Ltd for extracts from *A History of the English Church and People* by Bede translated by Leo Sherley-Price; Floris Books for an extract from Saint Margaret edited by Iain Macdonald; The Rt Revd Michael Hare-Duke, Bishop of St Andrews, for an extract of his hymn on St Margaret, the full text of the hymn is printed in *Hearing the Stranger*, Cairns Publications; Hyperion Records for an extract of Christopher Page's translation of a text from Hildegard of Bingen; The National Society for extracts from *Together for Festivals*, CIO, 1975 for Mothering Sunday.

Material from *The Alternative Service Book 1980* and *The Promise of His Glory: Services and Prayers for the Season from All Saints to Candlemas*, is reproduced by permission of the Central Board of Finance of the Church of England.

Cover and other illustrations by Julie Baines
Cover design by Shaun Evans, 2Q
Page design and typesetting by National Society/Church House Publishing

Print arranged by Indeprint Print Production Services

Printed by Bell and Bain Ltd., Glasgow

CONTENTS

INTRODUCTION

Festive Allsorts is a practical resource book packed full of ideas for celebrating the Christian year with children. It is designed for people who work with the under-11s in church groups, schools, midweek clubs, family services and those special one-off occasions.

Allsorts is the name of the *Church Times* children's page, and the chapters in this book have been selected from the articles which appeared in the *Church Times* between 1990 and 1994.

Festive Allsorts has 58 chapters on the major festivals and saints' days of the Christian year, loosely based on the ASB calendar. Special attention has been given to the Celtic saints.

Each chapter provides:

- background information on the saint or festival
- discussion questions
- all sorts of activity ideas

Some chapters also give suggestions for worship. The emphasis throughout is on learning through experience. Many of the activity suggestions have been contributed by diocesan children's advisers, Sunday school teachers, and children's workers from a wide variety of backgrounds.

How to use this book

Festive Allsorts is a resource book to dip into. Each chapter is self-contained and designed to provide story and craft ideas for a session lasting at least half an hour. There are activity suggestions for different age groups and some of these will need be to be adapted to suit your local conditions. Some activities will need advance planning so that the necessary materials can be collected before the session.

Safety

Great care has been taken to check that the activities in this book are suitable for children. But all the activities given need adequate adult supervision. Special care needs to be taken with activities that require cooking, modelling materials, the use of paint and varnish, sharp objects or small objects which could pose a threat if swallowed.

The 1989 Children Act specifies the amount of care and supervision necessary for children, particularly the under-8s. If the event you are planning will last over two hours and involves the care of under-8s then you must inform the local authority Social Services department.

Starline to Advent

I n Western Christendom Advent Sunday, the first day of the Advent season, is the Sunday nearest St Andrew's Day, 30 November. In the Eastern Church Advent is a longer season beginning in the middle of November. Traditionally Advent, like Lent, was kept as a period of fasting and penance: the solemn character of the season is marked by the liturgical use of purple.

Advent is a time of preparation for the coming of Christ at Christmas. It is also a season of getting ready and waiting for the coming of Christ's kingdom. Maintaining the season as a time of penitence and spiritual 'getting ready', as well as rehearsing the nativity play, practising the carols and making the Christingles presents a dilemma for anyone working with children. One way to maintain some of the distinctive character of the Advent season is to take the symbol of the star and show how it can help people prepare for Christmas'.

Stars have become a central prop in most respectable nativity plays. In the Gospel accounts of Jesus's birth, the star appears only in Matthew when the Magi tell King Herod that they have seen a star in the East and have come to see the King of the Jews. That same star leads the Magi to the house where Jesus was. The star is both a celesial sign, a portent that something great has happened and a guide. These activities explore star shapes as prayer pointers or guides.

Prayer stars

You will need card, foil paper, scissors, plates and a pencil.

Follow the diagram to make these simple stars.

1 Draw round a plate on the card. Using a smaller plate, draw a second circle within the first. Cut out round the larger plate outline.

2 Fold into four as shown in figure 2, and cut along the fold AE.

3 The ABC segment should be half the size of segments ACD and ADE.

   Cut along lines AC and AD.

4 Open out the circle to reveal 10 equal segments.

5 Open out every other segment to make five star points. These stars can be made of different types of card or card

with foil glued on to one side so that the shape catches the light. They can then be used in a number of ways.

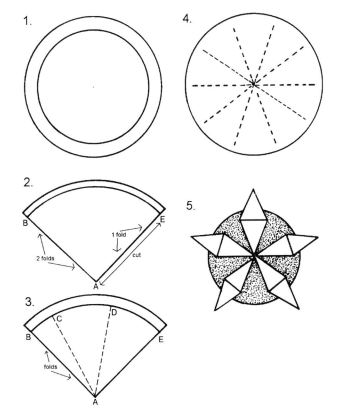

- Ask younger children to write a simple five-word prayer on the points of the star.
- Larger stars could be used by older children to think of five 'prayer pointers' throughout Advent or for the four Sundays of Advent and Christmas Day.
- Some might like to compose prayers on the stars and give them to members of the congregation as a present.
- Prayer stars from the whole group could be mounted on a wall behind a crib or nativity scene.
- A very large star cut-out could be mounted on a plain circular sheet of card. The 'five points' could become the doors of a 'five week' type of Advent calendar. The children could draw pictures behind each point or door as a focus for prayer. The doors can then be opened out on the appropriate day.

Star biscuits

Most children enjoy the food preparations for Christmas. Simple biscuits like those illustrated can be made by a group and then given as gifts to friends and family. You will need to have adequate adult supervision for the group.

For 24 biscuits you will need 4oz margarine, 6oz of plain flour, 1 egg, 3oz sugar, a teaspoon of ground cinnamon and half a teaspoon of ground mixed spice, rolling pin and star cutters.

1 Rub the margarine into the flour mixed with the spices.

2 Cream the egg with the sugar and stir into the flour mixture. (If time is short the teacher can prepare the dough before the session and keep it in a plastic bag in the fridge.)

3 Roll out the mixture to $1/4$" thickness and cut into star shapes using a cutter or cut out the template given and use this to cut around.

4 The biscuits can be decorated with sugar silver balls, jelly diamonds (not too many otherwise the star becomes a gooey mess) and chocolate polka dots.

5 Bake in an oven Gas Mark 4/180°C/350°F on a greased baking tray, or one lined with silicon paper, for 15 minutes or until golden brown.

6 Allow to cool on the trays.

The Saint Who Threw Money Around

ST NICHOLAS

6 DECEMBER

S t Nicholas is a universally popular saint, venerated in both East and West, by young and old. His patronage covers children, sailors, unmarried girls, merchants, pawnbrokers, apothecaries, perfumiers, bankers, scholars, parish clerks, Aberdeen, New York and Russia. He appears everywhere from Russian icons to Christmas cards. Being an adaptable figure, this great Christian saint has become immortalised in our secular culture as Santa Claus.

The life of this fourth century bishop of Myra is virtually unknown. Myra, modern Mugla, is in south-western Turkey. One tradition says Nicholas was imprisoned during the persecution of Diocletian.

His cult was established in the East by the sixth century and a fictitious biography of him by Methodius in the ninth century increased his popularity. It recounts many legends about the saint: his holiness is shown by the close affinity of his life to Christ's. Like Christ he performs miracles, stills storms, cares for the needy, suffers and dies.

The original Santa Claus

The most famous legend about him tells how he threw three bags of gold into the room of three daughters of an impoverished nobleman, thus saving them from prostitution. Other versions say that St Nicholas put the money in the girls' stockings at the end of their beds. This story is believed to be the origin of the pawnbroker's sign of three gold balls. It may also have given rise to the practice of hanging up stockings at Christmas, to the popularity of chocolate coins and to the custom of putting new coins into stockings.

In many parts of Europe, including Germany, Holland and Austria, St Nicholas visits the home of children near his feast day. Good children receive toys and sweets, naughty ones are given punishments by his companion whose identity differs from area to area. Children leave their shoes by the fireside before St Nicholas' Day and find them filled with sweets, fruits and nuts on 4 and 5 December. Dutch immigrants took their traditions to America. The Dutch St Nicholas, Sinterklaas, who was adopted in the New World eventually became the modern Santa Claus.

Telling the legends

The legends about St Nicholas bring together the Advent and Christmas themes of expectation, excitement, gift-giving and goodness. They provide a rich resource for the teacher. Retell some of the legends about St Nicholas. The story about how he stills a storm has been a favourite subject in Christian art. A class could do its own collage of this event using sponge-painting to create the sea with a card boat jutting out of the waves. Children could act out the incident when St Nicholas secretly gives gold coins to three poor women; or play a game trying to throw chocolate coins into three large Christmas stockings.

Bringer of gifts

St Nicholas is the great gift-giver and kind man. Explore the theme of gift-giving with the children. Ask them why gifts are given at Christmas and what they symbolise. Discuss with them whether they like giving presents and what sort of presents they choose for people. Encourage the children to consider what makes a gift precious. Then explain that St Nicholas gave gifts freely to those in need. He expected nothing in return.

FOR YOUNGER CHILDREN
Pass-the-parcel

Before the class prepare a pass-the-parcel. The parcel should contain a stocking full of sweets. After the discussion on gift giving play pass-the-parcel with the younger children. Ask the winner what St Nicholas would have done with the present. Would he have kept it for himself or shared it with the other children? It is hoped that the winner will get the message and share the sweets.

FOR ALL AGES
Make a gift shoe

Encourage the children to discuss the customs they have at home during Advent and Christmas. They will come to realise every home is different. Then explain some of the St Nicholas Day customs in Holland and Germany including how children leave out their shoes for St Nicholas to fill. The children can make their own paper or felt shoes to remind them of the custom.

You will need paper, colouring and decorative materials, stapler, scissors and small sweets, chocolate buttons or coins.

Get all the children to draw around their shoe on a piece of paper and cut out the outline. Then ask them to draw around the top part of their shoe on a second piece of paper and to cut this out. The top part of the shoe can then be stapled to the sole as shown in the diagram. Older children might prefer to use felt and sew the edges together. The children can decorate their shoes and fill them with small sweets to give to someone at home or in the congregation. They can write a greeting – Happy St Nicholas' Day – on the shoe or hang it up as a Christmas decoration.

Happy St Nicholas Day love Sarah

6

A Lighted Crown for St Lucy

St Lucy is one of those convenient saints about whom we know little, but whose memory brings together sound Christian themes with an excuse for a delicious food.

St Lucy lived in the fourth century. She was a native of Syracuse in Sicily. At the time of the Diocletian persecution she openly practised her Christian faith by distributing gifts to the poor. She was betrayed to the Roman authorities by a man to whom she had been betrothed by her parents, and was martyred in AD 303. St Lucy was venerated in the early church and Acts (stories) of her life exist from the fifth and sixth centuries, in Latin and Greek. Although the Acts are considered of dubious historical worth, an inscription dated about AD 400 survives in Syracuse and her popularity was established by the sixth century. In Christian art she often appears holding her eyes: these were said to have been torn out by her persecutors and then miraculously restored by God.

In Sweden, St Lucy's day on 13 December is a popular pre-Christmas festival. In each family a young girl is dressed in a long white robe girded with a red sash to symbolise martyrdom. She wears a crown of candles on her head. Early in the morning 'Lucia' visits family and friends distributing coffee and warm cakes. Some believe the tradition originated from the legend that St Lucy visited the persecuted Christians in the catacombs.

The name Lucy means 'light' and has the same roots as the words 'lucid' and 'translucent', so for children the festival can serve as a reminder of the theme of light. Some teachers might decide to link the festival with lighting Advent candles on an Advent Wreath. The candles symbolise the nearing of the festival of Christmas, when 'the light of Christ' appears.

There is a timing problem about using a yeast recipe in a short class session. The teacher could make up a packet of bread mix before the class for the group to add in fruit, chopped almonds (not to be eaten by very small children) and candied peel and shape the rolls during the session; but the rolls will still need between 20-40 minutes to prove. Traditionally the rolls are saffron flavoured and topped with sugar and served warm.

Alternatively the whole group could prepare a simple rock bun recipe. (Ensure that there is enough adult supervision for cooking activities.)

Blindfold games

St Lucy is the patron saint of those who suffer from eye diseases because of the legend about the miraculous healing of her eyes. Few children understand what it means to be suddenly made blind or to have sight problems. St Lucy's day might, therefore, be an appropriate time to remember the blind and partially sighted. You could play well-known blindfold games such as blind man's buff with the group. After they have played the game discuss with the group how blind people rely on their other senses because they cannot see.

A St Lucy crown

You will need cardboard, stapler, cardboard rolls, white paper, foil, colouring materials, scissors, glue.

Cut out a simple band from card, preferably corrugated cardboard, to fit the child's head. Cover the outside of the cardboard rolls with white paper. Attach a flame shape, made from coloured paper and foil, to the top of each of the rolls to form the flame. Then with staples attach each candle, facing outwards to the band. Staple the band together to form the crown (see diagram). Some children might like to cover the band with leaf shapes to form a leaf crown.

The children can then dress up as St Lucy with surplices girded with a red sash.

Saffronsbrod

In Sweden the girls who are Lucia for the day take a tray of Saffronsbrod with coffee to their family and friends. They often also visit local hospitals to present the food. Church groups might want to adapt this custom in their local area.

Jesse Trees for Christmas

Midway through Advent the panic rises. We often feel as we do before a plane is about to leave. It is too late to do any more preparations; all we can do now is wait for take off.

Many children's workers will have prepared Christingles, cribs and trees. The nativity play is rehearsed and everything is nearly in place. With so many good traditions around which focus on Christmas, it is all too easy to lose sight of the connectedness of Christmas with the rest of the year.

The ideas offered here are intended to supplement the more traditional customs and to enable children to see Christmas in its context – in the liturgical year and in the sweep of salvation history.

The Jesse Tree

Jesse Trees are designed to show the genealogy of Christ. The image of the ascending order of generations is inspired by Isaiah 11. With children a Jesse Tree can be used in Advent and at Christmas to illustrate the place of the Incarnation in the story of God's dealings with his people. In the book, *The Promise of His Glory – Services and Prayers for the Season from All Saints to Candlemas* (Church House Publishing, 0 7151 3738 7) there is a useful chapter suggesting how a Christmas tree can become a Jesse Tree and take on a liturgical character. The tree should be decorated with symbols which represent events or people in the history of salvation:

'The sun, moon or stars can represent the creation, an apple stands for the fall, an ark or dove for the flood, the burning bush for Moses . . . There can be an angel of the annunciation, a rose or lily for the Blessed Virgin, and various symbols for Christ, such as a fish or a star. The coloured balls which customarily hang on the tree can be painted with monograms symbolising Christ, such as XP or IHS.'

A Jesse Tree for under-11s

You will need a small dead tree branch, a small container filled with pebbles to secure the branch, a small tin of gold gloss paint, brushes, overalls, thin card, scissors, drawing materials, brightly-coloured paper, glue, string or gift ribbon (see diagram).

Adults should carefully supervise the older children as they cover a branch with gold paint, giving the 'tree' a new life, as a reminder of the new life that was given at Christmas. (The children need to wear overalls).

Then discuss with the group what they have celebrated and done through the year at church: Epiphany, Easter, baptisms, Christian Aid Week, patronal festivals, harvest, etc. Ask them to design or copy a symbol for each of these occasions and draw them on the pieces of card. The card symbols can then be coloured, decorated and cut out to hang onto the tree with gift ribbon. On top of the tree they can make a symbol for the nativity.

A paper-flora wreath

You will need card, colouring materials, felt, glue, scissors, red gift ribbon.

Most children are familiar with the Advent wreath or crown. The ring-shape of a wreath represents the eternal nature of God and his unending love for all people. This paper-flora wreath is more of a Christmas decoration than an Advent crown but the symbolism of the ring-shape and flora used remain the same. Like the symbols on the Jesse Tree, the different flora on the wreath can remind children of the other seasons of the Christian year.

Before making the wreath get the older children to explore the meaning of the flora used in Christmas decorations. Traditionally, evergreens are used in a wreath to represent both eternal life and constant faith. Wreaths often contain:

- Christmas roses, symbolising the nativity
- ivy, for happiness
- holly leaves and bright red berries, for the crown of thorns and blood of Christ
- rosemary, for remembrance
- laurel, for Christ's victory over death

A simple wreath decoration or wall-hanging can be made from a cardboard ring. This can be coloured in green or covered with green felt or green tissue paper. Children can then cut out cardboard or felt shapes of the flora and stick them onto the ring. The wreath can be decorated with a bow and hung up with red ribbon.

Stephen: The Church's First Martyr

With the focus of attention on Christmas, it is easy to overlook the feast day that follows it. The 'Feast of St Stephen' in '*Good King Wenceslas*' is most commonly referred to as Boxing Day. Yet St Stephen was the Church's first martyr, and his death had a profound effect on St Paul and the early Church.

All we know about St Stephen is contained in Acts, chapters 6 and 7. It is likely that St Stephen was a Hellenistic Jew. He was one of the seven men who were appointed by the Apostles to distribute goods to the poor (Acts 6.5); he did 'great wonders and signs among the people' (Acts 6.8).

Stephen's forthright teaching annoyed some Jews who accused him of blasphemy. He was brought before the Sanhedrin, where he made a courageous speech. Recounting Jewish history he said that God did not depend on the Temple. Christ, he said, was the prophet announced by Moses, and the Messiah whom the Jews had waited for. He then denounced his hearers for resisting the Spirit and for killing Christ, just as their fathers had killed the prophets:

You stiff-necked people, uncircumcised in heart and ears, you always resist the Holy Spirit. As your fathers did, so do you. Which of the prophets did not your fathers persecute? And they killed those who announced beforehand the coming of the Righteous One, who you have now betrayed and murdered.' (Acts 7.51-52, RSV).

Stephen's defence enraged the Sanhedrin, who arranged to have him stoned to death for blasphemy. According to Acts one of the witnesses of his stoning was St Paul. Stephen died confessing Christ and asking forgiveness for his persecutors. He was buried by 'devout men'.

Retell the story of St Stephen to the group. Some might want to act it out and recall the drama of Stephen's speech to the Sanhedrin.

Suffering for your beliefs

St Stephen is often depicted in Christian art holding a stone. The horror of Stephen's stoning has been transformed by church history into the glory of his witness. But stoning people to death still takes place today. As a New Year project older children could find out where in the world today people are persecuted for their faith and beliefs. They could invite a speaker from a local Amnesty group to come and talk to them about freedom of belief.

FOR YOUNGER CHILDREN
Making ripples

In Acts Stephen's martyrdom is shown as the first of many in the Church. The consequences of Stephen's life and martyrdom had a great impact on the early Church and especially on St Paul.

One way to illustrate this simply to young children is to fill bowls with water coloured with food colouring. Get them to drop different sizes of stones into the bowls and watch the ripple effect. What do they notice about the ripples? Do they end anywhere?

You can then talk about how the effect of great people like St Stephen is like a stone thrown into water and producing ripples. The ripple effect of St Stephen is still here today.

Discuss with the children what the ripple effect might be if they: bullied another child; helped someone in need; told lies; ignored something which was wrong.

FOR OLDER CHILDREN
Prayer stones

As he was dying, Stephen prayed to God for his persecutors. One way to encourage children to see prayer as part of everyday life rather than an occupation reserved for Sunday is to get them to carry around 'prayer stones' in their pockets. Every time they touch the stone they can think about prayer.

The stones need to be small smooth pebbles. Some children might prefer to collect a number of small pebbles and paint crosses or symbols of martyrdom on them. See diagram. These painted stones could be used as a focus to remember those who have died or who are persecuted for their faith.

Bringing Gifts Fit for a King

'Then, opening their treasures, they offered him gifts, gold and frankincense and myrrh.' (Matt. 2.11 RSV).

For children, the gifts brought by the wise men from the East are exotic and unusual. Paradoxically, the feast of the Epiphany, the manifestation of Jesus, has often become obscured by its own tradition; children are left puzzling as to the contents of the parcels the wise men brought.

The traditional interpretation holds that gold is for a king, frankincense for God and myrrh for him who is to die. The three gifts are seen to represent different aspects of the personhood of Jesus. This scheme has exerted a strong influence on the popular development of the Epiphany, though many scholars now doubt its validity. All agree, however, that the wise men bring gifts fit for a king. These activities are designed so that the children can be taken back to the story and have a hands-on experience of the gifts.

First explore the theme of gift-giving with the class. Discuss with the children what gifts they have received for Christmas.

Which is the most precious to them and why? What presents did they give? Then discuss why we give presents at Christmas. Ask the class what they would have bought a new-born baby; then what would be an appropriate present for a new-born king. Once you have made the connection between the gift-giving of the children and that of the wise men, move on to a discussion of the symbolism of the gifts given to Jesus.

FOR YOUNGER CHILDREN
A gift mobile

Younger children can then make a simple gift mobile to remind them of the discussion.

You will need enlarged copies of the gift template, a wire coat-hanger, thread, old magazines or catalogues, tinsel.

Each child can be given a number of the present templates to colour in. On the reverse side they can stick a picture of a present they would give to the infant Jesus. The children can either choose a present and cut it out from the magazines or draw the picture themselves.

The completed gifts can be strung up on the coat-hanger. The hanger can then be decorated with tinsel and hung up.

FOR OLDER CHILDREN
Gold, frankincense and myrrh

Gold: Explore the symbolism of the gifts brought by the wise men. The class can then make their own gold coins, look at a censer, and take part in a scent game. Gold was considered the most precious of metals, and therefore an appropriate gift for a king to symbolise his worldly prosperity (Psalm 72.15, and Isaiah 60.6).

Remind the class that during the offertory the collection is taken up as a sign of Christians offering of their wealth to God.

Children can make their own gold coins by using a gold or yellow wax crayon and rubbing over a variety of coins to get the image. These can then be glued together to form a two-sided coin.

Frankincense: Frankincense is a sweet-smelling gum, obtained as a milky exudation from the frankincense tree. It is a constituent of incense. Frankincense was used in Old Testament times in sacrifice and is mentioned with cereal offerings in Jeremiah 17.26. It is a precious sweet-smelling perfume and today its nearest modern equivalent is incense.

Incense is burnt in some churches using a thurible or censer. The rising smoke from the censer is a symbol of the prayers of the faithful going to God. It also helps engage the senses more fully in worship.

Whatever the church tradition the visual imagery of incense is a useful one to pursue with children. If possible take a censer into the class and show the children how it works. For the activity ask the children to make copies of the censer illustrated and in the lines of smoke write the names of those they want to pray for.

Myrrh: Myrrh is the resin of a species of balsam which grows in Arabia and India. It produces a pleasant aroma like frankincense. It was used in anointing and is also mentioned in connection with embalming in John 19.39. In the Old Testament kings were consecrated for their high office by having oil poured on their heads. The Hebrews believed that the rite imparted a special endowment of God's spirit. The gift of myrrh from the wise men serves as a reminder that Jesus is the anointed one.

Today anointing is still common in many Christian traditions. The practice shows that someone has been set apart for God and his service. Anointing someone with oil is often done at baptism, confirmation and ordinations. If possible show the children the oil used for anointing and discuss its use.

Frankincense and myrrh were both precious perfumes. To remind the children of this you could pay a scent game.

Collect ten distinctive-smelling items – cinnamon, bayleaf, garlic, etc., and put each in a matchbox with a small hole punched in it. The children have to guess what is inside each box.

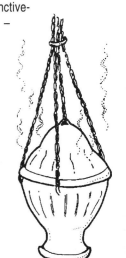

The Father of Monasticism

S t Antony of Egypt and St Pachomius are often regarded as the founders of Christian monasticism. St Antony is remembered in the ASB calendar on 17 January.

Antony was the son of a peasant farmer in Middle Egypt. A story of his life was written by St Athanasius, who tells us that when Antony was about 20 he responded literally to the reading of Matthew 19.21 and sold all his possessions and went to live among the local ascetics. First he lived in a cemetery and shut himself up in a tomb. Later he sought solitude in the mountains in the desert where he found an abandoned fort. Here he lived for 20 years.

Life in the desert was both a physical and a spiritual challenge. St Antony experienced a series of temptations, fighting with demons which showed themselves as wild beasts in the desert. These temptations became a favourite subject in Christian art. In 305 Antony organised a community of hermits to live under a rule of life. He tried to go back into solitude in 310; but by this time news of his miracles and spiritual greatness meant that many came to seek him out.

Towards the end of his life he withdrew into the Eastern desert to a mountain cave not far from the Red Sea. Followers of Antony and other ascetics led to a population explosion in the desert. St Athanasius wrote that the desert was made a city by the monks.

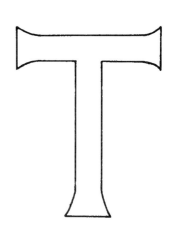

these near their special place to use. Discuss the idea of Bible-reading guides. Perhaps the group could start a lending library and share their books.

FOR YOUNGER CHILDREN
Journeys and prayers

Retell the story of St Antony. Explain that many people went on long journeys to visit Abba Antony. If possible take the group to visit someone who has a place of prayer in their house, or to a religious community where someone is able to explain the significance of their special place or chapel.

Make extra large copies of the template of the Tau Cross and give one to each child. Explain that St Antony and monks like him spent many hours in prayer. Ask them to draw in the cross the different times in the day when they might say prayers: morning assembly, grace at meals, bedtime prayers.

Very young children might enjoy constructing a cave and a model of St Antony from play-dough and putting it on a sand tray to remind them of his story.

Fourth-century asceticism is not an obvious subject to discuss with the under-11s. But St Antony did influence centuries of Christian monasticism and some of the sayings attributed to him can provide a helpful starting point for discussion with children.

Someone asked Abba Antony, *'What must one do in order to please God?'* The old man replied,

"Pay attention to what I tell you: whoever you may be, always have God before your eyes; whatever you do, do it according to the testimony of the holy Scriptures; in whatever place you live, do not easily leave it. Keep these three precepts and you will be saved.'

(From the *Sayings of the Desert Fathers* edited by Sister Benedicta Ward.)

FOR OLDER CHILDREN
St Antony's sayings

Retell the story of St Antony, explaining how he tried to follow God in the desert away from all the pleasures of life. Read out the saying of St Antony given above. Then take each phrase in turn as a starting point for discussion.

'In whatever place you live, do not easily leave it.'

Discuss with the group the importance of certain holy places: in church; in the countryside; on mountains or in a home. Do they know any holy places? Is there a place in their room where they pray to God?

'Always have God before your eyes.'

In the Coptic Church, people made icons depicting Jesus or a story from the Bible. Ask the group to make their own picture to put in their prayer space. Look at different religious paintings and icons for inspiration, and choose a story or verse from the Bible to illustrate.

Alternatively, the children can make a cross to put in their room. They could make this out of paper or from salt dough. They could make a Tau cross which is also known as St Antony's cross. See the template diagram.

'Whatever you do, do it according to the testimony of Holy Scriptures.'

Encourage the children to look at copies of children's Bibles or Bible stories and keep

Anglican Communion Sunday

In 1993 the Primates (the top bishops) of the Anglican Communion and the Anglican Consultative Council met in Cape Town, South Africa. Both bodies called for a day of prayer immediately before the meeting in January. Since then the day of prayer for the Anglican Communion has become an annual event in the calendar of Anglican Churches around the world.

Some years Anglican Communion Sunday falls immediately before the Week of Prayer for Christian Unity. These activity suggestions aim to help groups understand more about their own church before they take part in the ecumenical activities suggested in the next chapter on the Week of Prayer for Christian Unity.

The Anglican Communion is a family of 70 million people scattered in 160 countries around the world. Altogether there are 35 self-governing member churches or provinces. These churches are united by three things.

First, they have a common history. Second, they are in communion with the See of Canterbury and recognise the Archbishop of Canterbury as the principal Archbishop and the focus of unity within the Communion. Third, they have a common faith: they uphold the catholic and apostolic faith based on the scriptures and interpreted in the light of Christian tradition, scholarship and reason.

Churches of the Anglican Communion meet together on a regular basis. The Lambeth Conference of Bishops meets every 10 years and between these conferences there are meetings of Primates, and of bishops, clergy and laity at Anglican Consultative Councils, networks and regional gatherings. But informal meetings of the churches of the Anglican world happen all the time in parishes, through mission links, companion diocese arrangements, and visits of speakers from abroad.

The Compasrose map

The emblem of the Anglican Communion is the Compasrose. This symbol was designed in 1954 by the Revd Canon Edward West; the original wooden model of the emblem was made for the second international Anglican Congress in Minneapolis in 1954.

The centre of the symbol is the red cross of St George, a reminder of the origins and common history of the Church. The compass symbolises the world-wide spread of the Anglican faith. The mitre signifies the Apostolic Order which is essential to all the Churches in the Communion. Today the Compasrose can be found in many Anglican churches and cathedrals.

Younger children can colour an enlarged photocopy of the template illustrated. They can also stick the symbol in the centre of a sheet of paper and then make a collage around the Compasrose cut out from magazines of different faces to illustrate the variety of people in the Anglican Church.

A suitable all-age activity would be to make a Compasrose network poster. Mount an enlarged photocopy of the Compasrose on a large banner or sheet of paper. Then collect pictures of all the places and people the parish has links with around the world. Glue these pictures around the Compasrose and link with thread the pictures to the points of the compass to illustrate the world church links which already exist in the parish.

The Prayer links

Many churches of the Anglican Communion are united by using the Anglican Cycle of Prayer, which focuses on each diocese in turn.

Groups can use this Cycle of Prayer as a resource to find out more about the situation of different churches in the Communion. One way to make the prayer links visual is to use strips of sticky paper to form paper chains. On each link of the chain one person can write the name of a province or diocese. They can then find out more about that place and compose a prayer about it. These prayers can be written on the link itself or on separate pieces of paper. Once the links are joined together the completed prayer chain can be strung across an altar or around a display of the prayers and pictures done by the group.

Anglicans in action

There are a number of Anglicans who are well-known public figures – Terry Waite, Archbishop Carey, Archbishop Tutu, Hanan Mikhail-Ashwari. Older groups can have a competition during the the week before Anglican Communion Sunday trying to spot the number of times the Anglican Church or Anglicans are mentioned on the television, radio or in the newspapers.

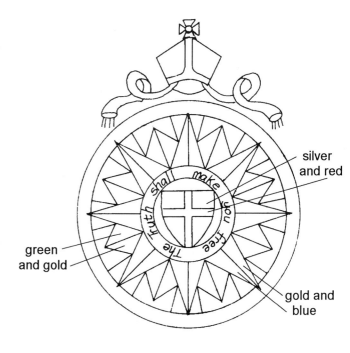

silver and red

green and gold

gold and blue

A Vessel for All Jesus's People

The Week of Prayer for Christian Unity is usually observed in England from 18 to 25 January: though some parishes prefer a week around Pentecost. Traditionally this is a time when different denominations come together for special services and prayer.

For children, the week can provide an opportunity to learn about other denominations and the vision of ecumenism. It could be the start of a term's project on studying other denominations.

By visiting different churches and talking to members of other congregations, children can begin to experience something of the diversity of Christianity for themselves and appreciate what is held in common between the different traditions. Before starting the activities teachers might do a Bible Study on John 17.21, where Jesus prays that his followers will be one so that the world will believe his Father had sent him.

FOR YOUNGER CHILDREN

All in the Boat

Give each child a copy of the template illustrated. Explain that 'OIKOUMENE' is the Greek word meaning 'whole inhabited earth'. The boat symbolises the church witnessing Christ to the world. At present the Churches are not united in their witness but the ecumenical hope is that one day all might be one so that the world may believe.

Younger children can use the ecumenical boat in a number of ways:

A badge

They can colour the template, mount it on card, attaching a safety pin on the reverse to make a badge to wear during the week.

An ecumenical boat

Alternatively, they might like to experiment by making their own ecumenical boats out of empty margarine tubs. The cross can be made by tying two lolly sticks together and attaching them in an upright position to the base of the boat with Blu-tak or plasticine. To illustrate the Christian family the children can make people figures out of playdough or plasticine to put in their boat, which they can sail in a washing-up bowl full of water.

A banner

Enlarge the template given and give a copy to each child. They can then colour in the symbol. They could cut out pictures of different people from magazines and glue them into the boat to make a collage. The finished symbol can be mounted onto a large sheet of card and made into a banner, using garden cane.

FOR OLDER CHILDREN

Ecumenical visits

During the Week of Prayer, arrange visits to other denominations in the area. These could be organised in collaboration with children's-work leaders in other churches to make the interchange fully ecumenical. Arrange in advance of the session for one person to explain about their church. Before the explanation get the children to explore the different churches for themselves. You could draw up a questionnaire for them to fill in:

What is the first thing they notice in the church? What is the most important part of the building? Can they find out what is the main service for this church? What type of decoration is around the church? By studying the notice-board, can they find out about the services and activities which go on in this church? What are the similarities between this church and their own?

If possible, arrange for the children to meet members of the Sunday school or a young people's group in the church they visit, or to be present for a service. After their visit the children can make a Week of Prayer scrapbook. This could include different accounts and pictures of the churches they visit.

All-age activity

For some churches, the Week of Prayer for Christian Unity provides the starting-point for discussion about other ecumenical activities: Lent groups, Good Friday services or Christian Aid Week.

If the children have met young members of different churches, they might arrange to do a regular activity together and invite adults to join them.

Some churches have arranged to do a passion play together or have a regular hunger lunch.

The Conversion of St Paul

S t Paul may be remembered on two days in the calendar. The Feast of the Conversion of St Paul is on 25 January. The Apostle also shares a day with St Peter on 29 June. As the June festival is more often associated with St Peter and ordinations, January is a good time for children to focus on St Paul. The Feast of the Conversion of St Paul is peculiar to the Western Church. In some early books about martyrs it is called the translation of St Paul, which suggests a date connected with moving his relics.

St Paul spent a considerable part of his life working for unity in the Church. So it is fitting that his festival comes at the end of the Week of Prayer for Christian Unity (18-25 January).

More is known about the life, work and theology of St Paul than any other character in the Bible. He was born in Tarsus in Cilicia, into a Hellenistic Jewish family of the tribe of Benjamin. He enjoyed the status of Roman citizen. We know from Acts that he was brought up a Pharisee (Acts 26.5), was educated in Jerusalem, and had a thorough knowledge of Judaism and the Law.

Acts also records that Paul persecuted the first Christians. He assisted at the martyrdom of St Stephen (Acts 7.58). It was after this, during a mission to Damascus to arrest Christians, that he was converted. No other conversion in the Bible is so dramatic or so well attested (Acts 9.1-19, 22.5-16, 26.12-18). This conversion convinced Paul of three things, which then dominated his future life: that Christ was alive; that God had called him to be an apostle; and that the purpose of his call was to bring the Gentiles into the new people of God.

Paul is one of the most influential figures of the early Church. His writings and theology have permeated all subsequent Christian theology. Some of this theology and the actual story of his conversion may be difficult for younger children to understand but there are many activities which can bring alive his change of beliefs, his missionary journeys and his persecution.

FOR YOUNGER CHILDREN
The body of the Church

The aim of this simple activity is to explore the metaphor of the body St Paul uses in 1 Corinthians 12.

You will need card or stiff paper, pencils, crayons, felt-tip pens, scissors, glue or sticky tape.

Divide the children into three groups and put them in different parts of the room. Ask the first group to choose one person to lie down on a large piece of card. Get the other children to draw around the child's head and torso. Ask the second group to do the same, but only to draw about the child's arms. The third group need to draw around the legs. Ask each group to cut out their drawing.

Bring the children together and ask the 'head and torso' group what a head and body can do on its own. Then ask the 'arms' group what arms can do on their own; and similarly with the 'legs' group. The children will realise the limited use of each part of the body if isolated from the rest.

Then go around the group asking each child what they are good at. Develop the idea that, if we use our individual abilities to help others, the group we belong to is stronger. Read the children 1 Corinthians 12 from a Children's Bible and discuss with them what Paul says about spiritual gifts and the body of Christ, the Church.

The parts of the body can then be glued or taped together to form a figure. Get the children to colour and decorate the figure so it represents a whole person.

FOR OLDER CHILDREN
An epistle to the PCC

Letters to children from international church conferences have become a popular way for Christian leaders to express their concerns in a simple way. Letters from children to church bodies are less common.

The aim of this activity is to get the children to consider St Paul's purpose in writing so many letters to different Christian communities and to decide what they would say in a letter to their own local church.

All you will need is some pens, paper and a Children's Bible.

Read out the first nine verses of St Paul's Letter to the Galatians from a Children's Bible. Ask the group to consider why St Paul wrote this letter to the Galatian Church. Ask each child to write a letter to their Parochial Church Council about what they see as the good things in their church and what they would like to change. It is important that the children receive a response.

Lights to Lighten the Days of Lent

The Presentation of Christ in the Temple is known by two other names, the Purification of the Blessed Virgin Mary and, more traditionally, Candlemas. The three titles give a clue to the three things being remembered on 2 February: the presenting and offering of a first-born Jewish child to God for his service; the Jewish rites surrounding childbirth for women (Leviticus 12.6); and the recollection of the prophecy of Simeon in the Temple that the infant Jesus would be 'a light for revelation to the Gentiles, and for glory to thy people Israel' (Luke 2.32 RSV).

The feast was first celebrated in Jerusalem in the fourth century. In 542 the Emperor Justinian ordered its observance at Constantinople as a thanksgiving after a plague; and then the custom spread through the East. A procession with candles is believed to have been added by Pope Sergius 1 (AD 687-701).

There are many customs associated with the season. It is often the time for blessing all the candles which will be used in church during the year, to remind Christians that they are to be 'lights to the world'.

Candlemas is not a straightforward festival to celebrate with children. It is probably not helpful to get bogged down in an explanation of Leviticus 12. Concentrate instead on the theme of light, the prophecy of Simeon that Jesus would be a 'light for revelation', and explore the imagery of candles.

A Candlemas calendar for Lent

This is similar to a modern Advent calendar but without the chocolate gifts which have become so common. You will need card, tracing or greaseproof paper, felt-tip pens, scissors and glue.

Get the children to draw doors on a piece of card, and on each door to draw a shape which represents a different type of light: stars, sun, moon, candles, light-bulbs, flames, lamps, lanterns. They can use an enlarged photocopy of figure 2 as a template. Make sure they leave the dotted line uncut, as this will serve as a 'hinge' for the Candlemas door.

The number of doors cut out depends on how you decide to use the calendar. Each child can make a door to open during each Sunday in Lent, or a door for each saint who has a day in Lent. A whole class could make a large calendar out of several sheets of card for each day in Lent. Once the calendar is cut out, get the children to glue tracing paper or greaseproof paper to the reverse of the sheet. Now the children can draw with felt-tip pens, on the paper behind the cut-out doors, pictures or symbols which help people see God's light in the world: a Bible, a saint, a self-portrait, the cross and so on.

The calendars can then be placed in front of a window for the light to shine through as each card window is opened during Lent.

Adapting the traditional customs

Some churches have a procession of light after the eucharist at Candlemas. This idea can be adapted in different ways for children or for all-age worship.

Saints have been examples of 'lights' for other Christians to follow. Ask the participants to choose the name of a saint, either someone from the past or someone living whom they consider a saint. The children could then learn about their chosen figures, and represent them in the 'candle' procession.

can then decorate the candle banner with shapes which depict the gifts they have which they can offer to God: a guitar shape for musical gifts, a runner for sporting gifts, etc.

At their baptism, children receive a candle as a sign that they are to be 'lights in the world'. Teachers can now make the link between these baptismal candles and the candle banners which illustrate how the children will use their God-given gifts. The candles or candle banners can be left in church and either lit or made visible every Sunday until Lent to remind the children of the theme.

Figure 2: Candlemas calendar and templates

A Candlemas banner

Figure 1: A candle-shaped banner

Candle-shaped banners can provide an alternative activity for teachers wary of children processing with lit candles. These can be made by children individually or in groups. Each candle shape can be drawn and cut out from a large sheet of card and attached on the back to a piece of dowelling. See illustration. The children

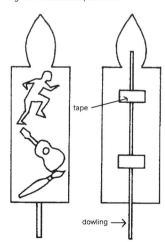

Parson-Poet of the Middle Way

George Herbert, the poet, priest and hymn-writer, is remembered in the ASB calendar on 27 February. At first reading the poems of this great Anglican divine are not an obvious choice for work with the under-11s but his anniversary could provide a focus for work on hymns and Christian poetry.

George Herbert was born in 1593 to an aristocratic family. He was educated at Westminster School and Trinity College, Cambridge. As a gifted classical scholar and musician, he seemed destined for the life of court. At Cambridge Herbert came under the influence of Nicholas Ferrar, the founder of the Little Gidding community in Huntingdonshire. Instead of the court he entered the ordained ministry, and was made Prebend of Leighton Bromswold near Little Gidding.

In 1630 Herbert moved to become Rector of Bermerton, near Salisbury. He was there for four years before his death of consumption in 1633. During his short priesthood Herbert gained a reputation for humility, energy and charity. His prose work *A Priest to the Temple: or the Country Parson* presents the sober and well-balanced ideal of an English clergyman.

There was a great flowering of the English language in Herbert's day. The priest's circle of friends included Francis Bacon and John Donne. George Herbert was one of the first devotional poets of the Church of England. He combined his priestly duties with the writing of some of the finest poetry in the English metaphysical tradition. Herbert had a profound influence on later Christian poets. Some of his poems have become well-known as popular hymns: *King of Glory, The God of Love my Shepherd is, Teach me, my God and King, Let all the world in every corner sing* (all in Hymns A & M and the English Hymnal).

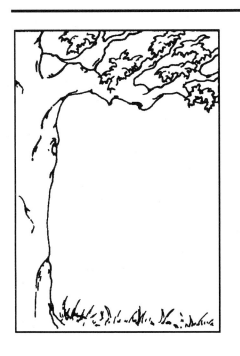

Hymn-singing

Talk to the group about their favourite hymns. Which do they enjoy singing and why? The word hymn comes from the Greek word meaning a song of praise of gods or heroes. Sacred poetry set to music and sung in church has always been part of Christian worship. Today hymns form an important part of many Anglican services, but this has not always been the case. Although George Herbert probably wrote *Let all the world in every corner sing* for singing in church, many of his other poems were only published as hymns at the beginning of this century. Use the first verses of three of Herbert's poems as the basis for activities with the group.

Let All the World In Every Corner Sing

Sing this hymn with the group. There are at least four tunes which are sung to this poem. If possible, sing the hymn to two different tunes and ask the group what feelings the hymn evokes in them? Which tune do they prefer and why?

The hymn first appeared in Herbert's book of poems entitled *The Temple*, and was designed to be sung antiphonally either by two choirs or a choir and congregation. Try this by asking one group to sing the refrain and the other the verse.

If possible take different recordings of Christian music from around the world for the children to listen to. Alternatively sing different styles of modern church music. Then ask the group to make a collage/poster to illustrate the opening of the hymn.

FOR YOUNGER CHILDREN

King of Glory, King of Peace

Sing the first verse of this hymn with the group. Explain to the younger children that George Herbert was a holy man who loved God and tried to show God's love in everything he did. A story about George Herbert is that he used to sit and meditate under a tree in his garden. If possible, take the group outside and ask them to look up into a tree and think about all the good things God has given them. Ask them to compose a prayer or poem of thanks to God. Give an enlarged copy of the tree template to each child and ask them to put their prayer in the space. Very young children can draw a picture in the space.

FOR OLDER CHILDREN

The God of Love my Shepherd is

Sing this hymn with the group. Herbert's poem was based on Psalm 23. Look up Psalm 23 in the Bible and read it out. Ask the group if they know of any other hymns which are based on this psalm. Discuss the imagery of the psalm with the group. Then ask them to compose a simple hymn or song which gives thanks for the way God looks after them. Use a well-known tune so that the group can concentrate on the words.

The Patron Saint of Wales

ST DAVID

1 MARCH

All we know for certain about St David is that he was Welsh, a monk, a bishop, and alive in the sixth century. Around these few facts a rich tradition has accumulated.

St David, or Dewi, was a saint of Pembrokeshire (Dyfed) on the western tip of Wales. After the Saxon invasion, Christians in the west and north of Britain developed links with Christians in Ireland, Gaul (France) and other Celtic communities. From Gaul came the monastic movement, which spread and flourished in Wales.

There were so many Welsh religious leaders in the fifth and sixth centuries that this period became known as the 'Age of the Saints'. Small monastic communities provided centres of Christianity and learning. Although St David is the most popular Welsh saint, the earliest written account of his life to have survived dates from long after his death. In about 1090 Rhigyfarch wrote a detailed biography which survives to this day in the British Museum.

According to this account David was the son of Sant, from a noble family, and his mother was Non, later to become a saint herself. David was first educated at Hen Fynyw and then studied for ten years as a priest under St Paulinus, the Welsh scribe. Rhigyfarch says the saint founded 12 monasteries, including Menevia, today's St Davids, and Glastonbury. David settled at Menevia, where the monks lived in extreme hardship following the example of those in Egypt. They tilled the land by hand plough, were allowed to speak only when necessary, and ate only bread, vegetables and salt. David's nickname was Aquaticus, because he and his monks drank only water.

David died at his monastery at Menevia and his relics are believed to be in St Davids Cathedral.

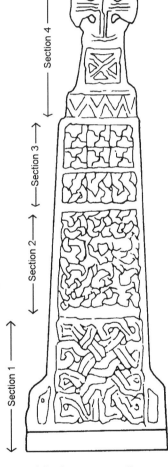

with the founder of a particular monastery. Later crosses became more elaborate, free-standing, with intricate carved detail. Celtic sculptors were influenced by Irish, English and later Viking art forms.

The Carew Cross, standing near the entrance of Carew Castle in Dyfed, illustrated here, is an excellent example of an eleventh century cross. These activities can help remind children that the crosses they see around the British countryside are linked to the foundation of the Christian faith in these islands.

1 In advance of the class, get two sheets of cardboard to draw a copy of the cross illustrated. Draw the design in felt-tip pen. Aim to have the cross as near to life size as possible (14ft). Cut out the different sections of pattern.

The older children can take sections one and two of the cross and stick coloured string or wool on to the design, following the continuous lines. Remind the group that the unbroken lines on Celtic crosses are said to symbolise eternity and the continuity of God's love.

Section three can be divided into smaller squares; each square can be given to a younger child to stick pre-cut wools on to the pattern areas. When the sections are completed they can be stuck on to a complete card cross and used as a focus for worship.

2 Photocopy enough copies of the crosses for children to colour in individually. Cut them out and stick them on to card for the children to use as bookmarks for their Bibles.

3 Get the children to copy some of the shapes on the Carew Cross, or other cross shapes, on to small stones.

A starting point for activities on St David is the collect in *The Cloud of Witnesses: A companion to the lesser festivals and holy days of the ASB,* published by Collins. 'Grant, O Lord, that as we give thanks for the life and work of your servant David, so your Church in Wales may faithfully preach the gospel which he proclaimed, and build on the foundation which he laid; through Jesus Christ our Lord.'

Giving thanks for the life of St David

St David is remembered for his preaching and teaching. He is the patron saint of a country renowned for its choirs, singers, musicians and poets.

After hearing the story of St David, children can be encouraged to prepare a special St David's Day service. The week before the class, ask the children to discover hymns, hymn-tunes, songs, music and poems written by Welsh people. Ask the children to consider

how St David preached the gospel. They could create a drama on this theme. Ask the older children whether a life as austere as St David's would be attractive today.

The children can then create a service which celebrates the life of St David. The service could include or focus on the Celtic cross made in the following activity.

Building on the foundation – the Celtic cross

The cross is now the universal symbol of Christianity; but it was some centuries before it became a popular symbol. Simple crosses carved on stones in Wales date back to the time of St David. These crosses showed that Christianity was established in an area. There might also be marked graves, a precinct of a monastery, or a place associated

Section 4 / Section 3 / Section 2 / Section 1

Following the Footsteps of St Chad

The primary source for our knowledge of St Chad, also known as Ceadda, is Bede's *A History of the English Church and People*. Chad was a native of Northumbria and a pupil of St Aidan at Lindisfarne. He also studied in Ireland. Like Aidan he travelled everywhere on foot and not horseback and according to Bede 'always sought to instruct his people by the same methods as Aidan and his own brother Cedd'. Bede tells us, 'He was a holy man, modest in his ways, learned in the scriptures, and one who was careful to practise all that he found in them.'

Chad became Abbot of Lastingham in north Yorkshire when his brother Cedd died. He was then, on the demand of King Oswy, made Bishop of the Northumbrians with his see at York. Oswy had become impatient at the absence of Wilfrid who had originally been appointed to the see but had gone to France to be consecrated.

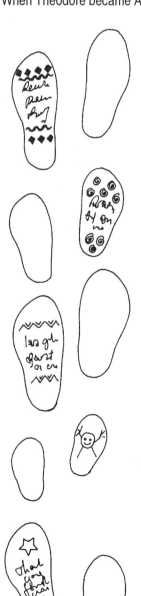

When Theodore became Archbishop of Canterbury he told Chad that his consecration had been irregular because Wilfrid had already been consecrated to that see. There was also some suspicion about the three bishops who consecrated him. Chad willingly offered to resign his office; he said he had never thought himself worthy of it. Theodore was so impressed by Chad's humility that he assured him that he would not be deprived of his office.

Later Archbishop Theodore made Chad Bishop of Mercia. Theodore also commanded that Chad ride on horseback whenever he took a long journey: 'The Archbishop,' Bede says, 'who recognised his outstanding holiness and considered it more proper for him to ride, himself insisted on helping him to mount his horse.' Chad established his see in Lichfield and built himself a house which he shared with seven or eight other men for prayer and study. He travelled widely and established a monastery in Barrow in today's south Humberside. According to Bede, Chad was forewarned by the 'heavenly company' of his imminent death. He died on 2 March 672 and was buried in Lichfield.

St Chad was a humble man who lived a life of prayer. In Lichfield he had a special oratory, or place of prayer, where he and his friends went to read and pray as often as possible.

Footsteps to prayer

You will need pens, paint, brushes, scissors, glue, sheets of paper and a roll of old wallpaper.

This activity can be for everyone in the church and might be used as part of a service. Divide the group into pairs and ask each child to draw around the feet of their partners. Cut these shapes out and colour them. Then remind the group that Chad preferred to walk everywhere on his missionary journeys. His long walks enabled him to meet people and to pray about them. Ask the group to think of people they want to pray for. They can then compose a short prayer and stick it on to one of the foot outlines. The feet can then be stuck on to the long roll of paper, and become a footpath of prayer for use in a service.

A prayer mobile

You will need wire coat-hangers, thread, drawing materials, card and scissors.

The group will need to choose a theme: 'Thank you, God', 'God's promise for me', 'Prayers for people I know'. Ask the group to draw pictures or find photographs to illustrate their theme. On the reverse of the pictures, older children might like to write a short prayer. The pictures can then be tied with cotton thread to the coat-hanger and hung as a mobile in a place where they can be an aid to prayer.

A place of prayer

Chad was from the Celtic tradition which believed that every aspect of daily life was invested with religious significance. God was not distant, he was immanent. One way to help a group understand the idea of prayer as a continual activity is for them to go on a walk. Ask the group to look around them and find things which reflect the glory of God. They might collect different items or draw them. Discuss with them how the things they have chosen reflect God's glory. These objects can then be displayed in a place they have set aside for prayer.

The Patron Saint of Ireland

ST PATRICK

17 MARCH

There are many stories about the patron saint of Ireland. Some are true, some are legend and some have a touch of the blarney about them. We can however be nearly certain that we are hearing the real St Patrick when we read the *Confession* or his *Letter to Coroticus* both of which scholars believe to originate from the saint himself.

Patrick was born between 390 and 414 in Britain. In the *Confession* he said his family owned a villa at a place called Bannavem Taberniae (possibly in modern Cumbria). He was the son of a local town councillor and deacon. When he was 16 Patrick was captured by Irish pirates. He was taken to work on a farm near 'the woods of Foclut by the western seas' probably in Co. Mayo. After the relative comfort of his home the shock of working as a shepherd in a remote country had a profound effect on him. He believed that he deserved his banishment because 'we turned away from God, and did not keep his commandments'. In his loneliness Patrick came to know God as a friend and companion.

After some years Patrick returned to England and was ordained. In a dream he received a call to return to Ireland to serve its people.

For the rest of his life Patrick devoted himself to bringing the Christian message to both chieftains and ordinary people. Chieftains entrusted their children to him so that he could educate them. These pupils travelled with Patrick as he went around Ireland evangelising, reconciling quarrelsome chieftains, ordaining clergy and setting up religious houses for monks and nuns. Patrick is believed to have died in about AD 460. Later legends of the great miracle-worker who expelled snakes from Ireland explain why Patrick is associated with so many towns and cities throughout the country. A particularly useful book for children on St Patrick is *The Real Story of Patrick* by George Otto Simms, the late Primate of All Ireland, (The O'Brien Press 1991).

These activities aim to help children relate St Patrick's story, and teaching associated with him, to their own experience.

A place collage

St Patrick was snatched away from his home and taken away to a land where he knew no one. In order for the children to appreciate the turmoil St Patrick might have faced ask them to think of occasions when they have had to had to leave a place they loved: starting school, moving house, the end of a holiday, and so on. Discuss with them their feelings on that occasion.

Ask the children to draw or write about their special places. You can mount the finished work on a collage.

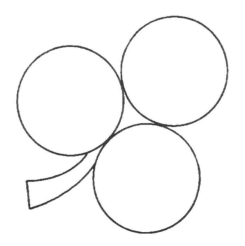

A Patrick bookmark

Saints are people through whom God's light shines. If possible read the children excerpts from Patrick's *Confession*. Then ask them to design a bookmark from card or material. On one side of the bookmark they should illustrate a symbol of light and on the reverse draw a picture of Patrick – a light in the world.

FOR OLDER CHILDREN
A breastplate prayer

Nearly 500 years after his death a life of Patrick was written in Irish: it was called *The Tripartite Life*. In it is the text of a prayer which has been associated with the saint. It is known as *St Patrick's Breastplate, The Lorica of St Patrick* or *The Deer's Cry*, and is found in many hymnbooks. Although many scholars believe that this was not written by the saint himself, the words in it echo Patrick's feelings and experience.

Sing Mrs Alexander's translation of the hymn with the class. Discuss with them why it is called a breastplate. What is it that they would call upon God to protect them from? Then encourage the children to make their own breastplate prayer.

FOR YOUNGER CHILDREN
A shamrock potato print

No activity page on St Patrick would be complete without a shamrock. The linking of St Patrick's teaching on the Trinity with this variety of clover first appears in written form in the eighteenth century. Simple teaching on the Trinity is hard to come by, and for each generation of children the shamrock is a new symbol.

Children can make their own shamrocks. You will need half a potato for each child. Try to make sure the potato halves are round in shape. The children can then print in paint three separate circle shapes to make a shamrock as shown. Remind them that the three circles represent the Father, Son and Holy Spirit and they come together to form one – the Trinity.

The potato prints can be made into a design or banner for St Patrick's day.

St Joseph and the Holy Family

The church remembers St Joseph, the husband of the Virgin Mary on 19 March. Although there is a wealth of apocryphal literature about St Joseph, his presence in the New Testament is limited to the infancy narratives of Matthew and Luke.

The New Testament tells us that Joseph was a pious Jew of Davidic descent. His family belonged to Bethlehem, David's city, but he lived in Nazareth (Luke 2.4), where he was a carpenter, (Matt. 13.55). The texts also tell us he was a kindly man (Matt. 1.19). He helped bring up Jesus for at least the first 12 years of his life (Luke 2.33, 41-42, 48).

After the visit to the Temple in Jerusalem, Joseph does not appear in the Gospel narratives. From the *Protevangelium of James*, an apocryphal infancy narrative dating from the second century, Joseph is depicted as an old man when he married Mary. A Greek document entitled The History of Joseph the Carpenter (fifth/sixth century) was important in establishing a cult of Joseph which probably originated in the East and developed in the West much later. His feast day was introduced into the Roman Calendar in 1479. Theresa of Avila and Ignatius Loyola both helped to spread his popularity. Joseph is the patron of fathers, families, bursars, procurators, manual workers, carpenters and all who desire a holy death.

top of the hat. A longer set to fit around the middle of the hat, and a set to fit around the bottom of the hat.

On the set of three dollies the children should draw the figures of Mary, Joseph and Jesus and then stick them around the top of the hat. On the middle set they should draw pictures of their own family and then glue these underneath the Holy Family. On the bottom set they should draw pictures of people in the church they know: the vicar, their teacher – their church family. Glue this set around the bottom of the hat (see illustration). Attach ribbons to tie underneath the child's chin.

Remind the children that Jesus and the example of the Holy Family are an example to everyone. The hat also reminds them that their family is part of Christ's family of the Church.

FOR OLDER CHILDREN

A day in the life of Joseph

For these activities the leader will need to take in books which explore the historical, social and geographical background of the New Testament, and a Bible atlas.

Discuss with the group how Joseph cared for his family when they fled from Herod to Egypt. Ask the group to draw a map which traces the route the Holy Family might have taken. Ask them to think about the dangers they might have faced from bandits, wild animals and natural hazards. Encourage the children to look up the appropriate chapters in the books you have brought in.

Ask the children to imagine a day in the life of the boy Jesus with Joseph and his family in Nazareth. Again encourage the children to use reference books.

Get the group to write their own playlet about this Nazareth day.

FOR ALL AGES

A prayer family history

Joseph and Mary needed their loving and obedient relationship with God throughout their life journey as a family. One way to illustrate a family life journey is to make a prayer history book.

This could be done in a loose-leaf book with illustrations of each family member. At different times different members of the family, separately or together, could compose particular prayers for each other. The album could include photographs and souvenirs to reflect the moments of prayer a family makes for its members through life, from birth, baptism, early years through to sickness and dying.

FOR YOUNGER CHILDREN

Family hats

The children will need adult help and supervision with this activity.

Make a conical hat out of card ensuring that the rim fits the child's head. Make sets of paper dancing dollies. The height of the dollies should be just under a third of the height of the hats. Give each child three sets of dollies: one set of three to fit around the

The Missionary who wanted to be a Hermit

Northumbria is home to many saints, but Cuthbert stands out as a giant among them. An energetic missionary, miracle-worker, prophet, and ascetic during his lifetime, he has increased in fame and popularity since. There are many lives of Cuthbert: the earliest was written by an anonymous monk of Lindisfarne in about 700. It was shortly followed by lives written by Bede.

The story of Cuthbert as recounted by Bede retains so much of its original directness and immediacy that older children might enjoy reading parts of it for themselves.

As a youth Cuthbert entered the monastery of Melrose in 651 under Abbot Eata. Eata sent him to Ripon; but in 661 he returned as prior to Melrose, where he trained many men 'with masterly authority and by his personal example'.

Cuthbert was a great missionary. Like Aidan, his predecessor, he travelled on foot to the outlying areas, going into the mountains 'which others feared to visit'. Bede gives a clear indication of the saint's holiness: 'Cuthbert was so skilful a speaker, and had such a light in his angelic face, and such a love for proclaiming his message, that none presumed to hide their inmost secrets, but openly confessed all their wrongdoing; for they felt it impossible to conceal their guilt from him.'

Cuthbert was sent to Lindisfarne to instruct the monks there and to restore regular discipline. Although he came from a Celtic background, after the Synod of Whitby 664 he adopted Roman customs and had to persuade the Lindisfarne monks to do the same. Cuthbert was drawn to the life of a hermit: from Lindisfarne he moved out onto an adjacent island, which is today known as St Cuthbert's Isle, and then to Inner Farne, where he lived in almost complete solitude. But church and secular leaders had other plans for him, and elected him Bishop of Lindisfarne. Cuthbert could not be persuaded to take up the post until King Egfrith and others came and begged him.

After two years as a bishop, when he undertook many missionary journeys, Cuthbert returned to his island hermitage, 'God having made known to him that the day of his death was drawing near'. Cuthbert died on Farne Island on 20 March 687 and was buried on Lindisfarne. Eleven years after his death his body was elevated so that a new shrine could be built. When the coffin was opened, Bede records, Cuthbert's body was 'uncorrupt as though still living'. It was at this time that Eadfrith (696-698) wrote and decorated the Lindisfarne Gospels in Cuthbert's honour. Many miracles are associated with Cuthbert's tomb and relics. His relics found their permanent home in Durham in 995.

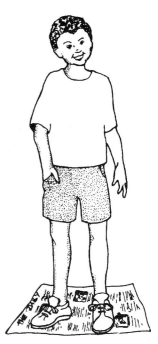

Creating an island

Cuthbert wanted to live the life of a hermit on a deserted island. Discuss with members of the group why he wanted to do this. To help the group think about Cuthbert's life they can do a number of island activities:

1 Give a sheet of newspaper to each child. Ask them to put their sheets together to create an island. The idea is that they dance around the island until the music stops, when they jump on it. The last one to jump on the island is out. When a child is out they take a sheet of newspaper away from the island so that the island gradually becomes smaller. At the end of the game only one child is left on a small island. Ask that child to explain the difference between a crowded island and an empty one. The leader can adapt this game in a number of ways to lead into a discussion about living on islands.

2 The group could also make their own island models from round cheese boxes or cardboard cut-out shapes stuck onto an imaginary sea.

3 Arrange the group into a circle with everyone looking out. Ask them to be silent and imagine they are each on an island. What do they think about? Would they like to be alone on an island?

After doing one of these activities ask the group to consider the qualities of an isolated island. Why might an island be conducive to prayer?

Prayer as a continual activity

Cuthbert came from the Celtic tradition which believed that God was concerned with all aspects of life. Celtic people offered prayers at every point of their day – from rising in the morning, laying the fire, milking the cows, grinding the corn, cooking and eating to going to bed at night. Everything they did was an occasion for prayer, for inviting God into their activities and work and for finding God's presence.

For many children the idea of 'arrow prayers', or saying grace before a meal, might be a way in which this tradition can be explored. Ask the group to compose graces for breakfast, lunch and tea. Discuss with them why we say grace. What do they have to be thankful for at different stages of the day and what do they ask for?

How Lent need not be all Doom and Gloom

Lent has long been observed as a season of preparation for the great events of Holy Week, Good Friday and Easter. The 40 days that recall the period which Jesus spent in the wilderness (Luke 4. 1-14) begin on Ash Wednesday – 40 days before Easter, not counting Sundays.

The themes of Lent

The themes of Lent can be summarised as self-denial, penance and prayer. During early Christian history the observance of the Lenten fast was very strict. Only one meal a day was allowed. Meat, fish and in many places eggs and milk were forbidden. The names given to the days before Lent all date back to the Christians' 'final fling' before the season of austerity. 'Shrove', in 'Shrove Tuesday', comes from the word 'shrive' – 'give penance' and hence absolution, traditionally the day when people went to church to confess their sins. 'Pancake Tuesday' takes its name from the custom of making pancakes and using up all the fine flour, eggs and milk in a household before Ash Wednesday. 'Mardi Gras', literally 'fat Tuesday', is traditionally the day when fats were eaten up. 'Carnival' is probably derived from the Latin 'carnem levare'– to put away fresh meat.

Today the pancakes, processions and carnivals remain, but in the Western Church the strict Lenten fast has become rare. Prayer and spiritual renewal have always been part of the Lenten tradition and remain central to Lenten observance. Ecumenical Lent groups and Bible study groups, Lent books and special services are more common today than specific spiritual exercises.

Children should not fast, but it is possible to explore the theme of self-denial with them. Ask the children to decide what it is that they really enjoy: sweets, canned drinks, television, videos. Could these be limited during Lent? Could the money or the time saved be used in a positive way? You can look at the positive aspects of 'giving up' by 'doing things for God' and turning Lent into TaLent time.

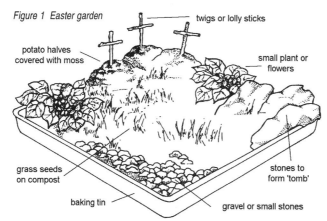

Figure 1 Easter garden

- twigs or lolly sticks
- potato halves covered with moss
- small plant or flowers
- grass seeds on compost
- stones to form 'tomb'
- baking tin
- gravel or small stones

and the children can come to see how 'giving up' can be a positive and creative exercise.

Talent time

In the parable of the talents, in Matthew 25, Jesus speaks of servants being entrusted with talents to use in the master's service. It is possible to capitalise on the double meaning of talent by inviting children first to identify what positive talents each may have: skills at a ball game, cooking, friendship – the list is endless. A good way of doing this is to get them to talk in pairs and each identify a talent in the other. The children can then think of ways in which they can 'give up' their talent, by using it to help someone else – getting sponsorship for a local swim to help those in need. During Lent, progress can be reported

Increasing talents

The talent can be taken more literally and each child be given ten talents or 10p pieces and asked to make ten talents more during Lent by doing something with the money: buying ingredients for a cake to be sold for profit; buying sheet music for a sponsored piano play. At the end of Lent the 'TaLents' can be donated to charity.

Activities using the readings for the First Sunday in Lent

The Old Testament lesson for the first Sunday in Lent Year One is Genesis 2.7-9, and Genesis 3.1-7, the creation and the fall.

After reading the stories to the children, teachers can draw out the theme of the right stewardship of God's earth. These activities help children understand how God's earth is misused and how they as individuals and as a group can bring about small but important changes.

FOR YOUNGER CHILDREN

An Easter garden

Collect the materials you will need to help children make an Easter garden. The size and shape of the garden depends on the group (see illustration for suggestions). In the first week sow grass seed. Throughout Lent encourage the children to water and look after the garden. Ask the children to think of examples of places which are not cared for at home, in their local park, or at school. Get them to consider how they can say 'sorry' to God for not caring for his world and his people.

FOR OLDER CHILDREN

A tree-of-life poster

You will need a large sheet of card, paper, drawing materials, scissors and glue or sticky tape.

Discuss with the group ways in which the world is misused. Then get them to consider how they need to change as individuals and as a community to make the world a better place to live. Draw an outline of a tree on a piece of card in advance. Ask each child to draw round their hands and cut out the drawing. Then get them to cut out a newspaper cutting, write a short paragraph or draw a picture on each hand to illustrate how they can become more caring of God's world. The hands can then be stuck on to the tree of life. (See illustration).

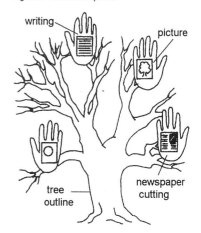

Figure 2 Tree-of-life poster

- writing
- picture
- tree outline
- newspaper cutting

Mothering Sunday

Traditionally, Mothering Sunday, the fourth Sunday in Lent, was a time when people visited their mother church or cathedral. From the eighteenth century the festival came to be the day when people in domestic service visited their own mothers. Today Mothering Sunday celebrates both mother church and our own mothers and carers.

When people lived in settled communities, the village outing to the local mother church or cathedral was a big event. Mothering Sunday today could still provide the occasion for a parish trip to a cathedral; but it can also provide a time for reflection on how the local church is mother.

One way to do this was suggested by Alan Beck in *Together for Festivals* (CIO Publishing 1975). One year he found he had a baptism service booked for Mothering Sunday, so he called on the family concerned to help him in a special celebration. During the service he drew the parallels between the life of a new-born baby and the care it receives, and the birth and nurture of a new member of the church. A teacher can develop this idea to suit her own group. If possible ask new parents to come and help you and bring in suitable props: a hospital label for a baby, a bath, an ABC chart, and so on. The following parallels can then be drawn and discussed with the children:

● the labelling of a new-born baby in hospital and declaring the Christian name at baptism

● the baby's first bath in hospital and the spiritual washing at baptism

● the baby's new clothes and christening robes, symbolising new life

● the baby's feeds and the spiritual food of prayer

● the quick learning of a baby and learning about the Christian life

● the people who help new parents, the health visitor and others who help the baby stay healthy and the godparents and parents who help the baby grow up strong in the faith

The gift-card combines a Mothering Sunday gift with the idea of mother church. First discuss with the children how a church is 'mother' to them. The second activity explores the idea of the family of the church.

A Mothering Sunday gift card

You will need soft fimo for younger children, fimo, safety-pins, PVA glue, brooch holders, card, scissors, plenty of adult supervision.

When apprentices or those in domestic service went home to visit their mothers on Mothering Sunday they would often take flowers, cakes, a trinket or a brooch. Children can make a brooch for their own mothers from fimo. These will need to be made the week before Mothering Sunday so that the teacher can bake the fimo to harden it during the week. For cooking times follow the instructions on the packet. Younger children can make their brooches out of soft fimo. They can mould a simple shape and prick out their mother's initial with a pencil. Once the brooches are baked the teacher can stick on a safety-pin with PVA glue. Older children can be given a number of colours to work with and produce their own designs. They can also use safety-pins or the ready made brooch-holders which are available from craft shops.

A Mothering Sunday card can be made in the shape of a church. All the children should draw the outline of their own church, making sure doors are central to their picture. Cut the doors so that they open to reveal the inside of the card. In this space attach the brooch. See diagram. Add a greeting to the card.

A church family collage

Another avenue to explore on Mothering Sunday is the idea of the church family. When families used to go and visit their mother church or cathedral on Mothering Sunday they would usually live in the same area. Today families are often geographically separated but they may still be united by their church-going. The week before Mothering Sunday ask the children to bring in photographs or pictures of churches their families are linked with – where their parents were married, where a relative was christened, confirmed or buried or where they have been to church on holiday. On a large map, discover where your local church has links. Put a picture of the local church on the map. Give each child a piece of thread, and ask them to put their picture near the appropriate place on the map and link it to the picture of their local church with the thread. The children can then create a banner for their map – Our Church Family.

The Drama of Palm Sunday

Palm Sunday, the day on which palm crosses are blessed and distributed throughout the congregation, marks the beginning of Holy Week. Many churches have a special procession on Palm Sunday as a reminder of Jesus's triumphal entry into Jerusalem. This Allsorts explores how the traditional procession can be modified to create an all-age Palm Sunday drama.

Read out an account of the entry into Jerusalem in St Matthew's Gospel (21.1-11), or ask one of the children to read it. Now ask the children to close their eyes and imagine that they were one of the crowd shouting 'Hosanna' as Jesus went by. Discuss with them what they would have felt if they had been there. Ask them to imagine they are one of the disciples and describe their reaction to the scene. These exercises can be done in preparation for the drama so that the children become familiar with the story.

These suggestions are for an all-age drama on Palm Sunday with time for preparation with a children's group the week before.

FOR YOUNGER CHILDREN

Donkeys and palm trees

The week before Palm Sunday the younger children can make crowns, palms and a donkey for use in the drama. For crowns you can staple together cut-out leaves to create a palm crown or make a more conventional kingly crown which the children can decorate with collage materials.

The palms can be made from large sheets of green paper or newspaper. Roll up a large sheet of paper at least A4 size (newspaper works well) to make a long tube. Secure the tube with sticky tape. Make cuts downwards at one end of the tube as shown in the diagram. Gently pull the cut paper tassles from the centre of the tube, holding the base securely to create a bunch of palm leaves.

For the donkey, map out a grid on a large sheet of paper. Then copy the template given within the enlarged grid. If possible make the donkey life-size and strengthen the paper with a cardboard backing. Once you have the outline, the children can create the donkey fur by filling in the outline with stuck-on screwed-up pieces of tissue paper or newspaper. Attach a piece of card in the middle of the back of the donkey so that the children can hold the model on the reverse to process into church for the drama.

FOR OLDER CHILDREN

Banner making

The same week, older children can prepare banners to be held by crowd members. Discuss with the group what banners a modern crowd would hold if a famous person

came to town. The banners for Palm Sunday might include the captions like 'Jesus is King', 'Jesus, Son of God', 'Prince of Peace', 'Son of David rules OK', 'There's only one Jesus', and so on.

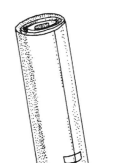

A news report

Ask the group to write a report of the event for the *Jerusalem Times* from different viewpoints: as a member of the crowd, one of the disciples, Jesus.

During the drama itself the group could choose a number of children as television and radio reporters to interview members of the crowd for an evening news bulletin.

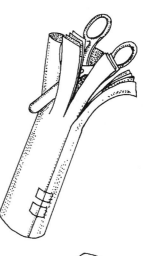

All-age drama

When the props have been made, arrange a re-enactment of the scene itself. The week before the drama, decide who is going to be Jesus, the donkey carrier, the disciples, the reporters, and the various other participants.

Ask the crowd to bring their own props, including rattles, with football hats and scarves and coats to throw on the ground.

Some groups might want to write down the play, others might prefer to extemporise. Suitable music could be added.

After the drama, make time for the group to come together to discuss the presentation. Ask them again what it felt like to be a member of the crowd, a disciple, or Jesus. Has the play made a difference to their understanding? What did they see? What did they feel about Jesus?

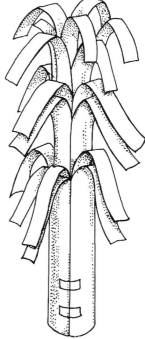

Celebrating Easter

The celebration of the resurrection of Christ is the greatest festival in the Church. It is the commemoration of Christ's victory of life over death. In the Western Church Easter Day falls on the Sunday following the first full moon after the spring equinox on 21 March. Easter Day can therefore fall between 21 March and 25 April.

The name Easter probably owes its origins to the ancient spring goddess 'Eostre'. Bede thought that this was so, and it is clear that the Christian festival superseded an old pagan festival.

These activities explore the themes of Easter of celebration and new life.

FOR OLDER CHILDREN
The tomb: stone-painting

Read the introductory sentence for Easter Day from the Alternative Service Book to the group: 'On the first day of the week the disciples went to the tomb, and they found the stone rolled away from the tomb. Alleluia!' (Luke 24.1.)

Ask the children to act out the scene of the first Easter morning from St Luke chapter 24. Ask them to imagine what the reactions of the women would have been when they found the stone rolled away from the tomb. Would they have been frightened, excited, happy or worried? What would the children think if they had seen the stone rolled back? Would they guess that Jesus was alive again?

Take a collection of smooth pebbles and rocks in to the group. Using acrylic paint and fine paint-brushes, the children can draw a symbol or a word on the pebbles to express the joy of the first Easter. (Ensure that there is enough adult supervision for this activity and that the children have aprons or overalls on.) These decorated pebbles could form part of an Easter garden or a display in church.

New life: a green cross

It is not easy to discuss the resurrection in conceptual terms with children. However, they are familiar with many experiences in life which can serve as useful analogies in opening up the theme. Talk about the disciples' amazing discovery: that Jesus's death was not the end. They now understand more clearly the purpose of his life and his ministry: to bring the whole universe back to

God. In meeting the risen Lord they too received his gift of new life.

Discuss with the group their experience of new life or new beginnings: a baby, a puppy or other pet, eggs, spring, flowering bulbs; or, with older children, moving house or moving to a new school.

With younger children talk about things around them which might look dead but have new life within them: eggs, twigs, seeds, chrysalises, and so on. If possible, go out with the group to collect items to put on a new-life nature table.

To illustrate the idea of new life at Easter many churches make Easter gardens. In addition to planting an Easter Garden, young children might enjoy watching how seeds grow and develop. The children could plant beans, peas or cress seeds in a cross shape during Lent. Encourage them to look after the seeds. When the seeds have sprouted, talk about how the seeds were, how they looked dead until they were given the right conditions to grow. Go on to explain that Easter is a special day because we remember that Jesus, who died on Good Friday was raised to new life again on Easter Day.

FOR YOUNGER CHILDREN
An egg-tree

The origin of the Easter egg is uncertain. The custom of giving eggs can be traced back to ancient China, where eggs were decorated and used to signify the return of spring and the continuance of life. For Christians the egg became a symbol of the resurrection of Jesus and new life. Egg decoration is a common custom throughout Europe. In some countries decorated eggs are hung on a flowering branch as a reminder of the new life of Jesus. Unless you are partial to omelettes, egg decoration can be a bit hazardous for the very young, but the custom can be adapted to suit them. In advance of the session prepare enough paper egg-shapes for each child to have one. Pisanki eggs, the highly decorated eggs common in Poland, are made by drawing a wax design on the egg and then dyeing it in vegetable dye. Younger children can create a similar effect by crayoning their paper egg-shape with a pale wax crayon. Then they should use a dark colour and crayon over the pale shade. Using a blunt pencil or a coin they can then scratch out a design on the egg so that the pale colour is revealed. Using thread, hang these eggs from a flowering branch as a decoration for Easter.

The Patron Saint of England

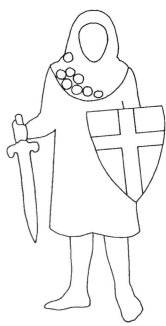

W ho was this knight in shining armour who captured the imagination and hearts of Christians in both East and West?

We know very little about the real St George. It is likely that he lived in the fourth century and suffered martyrdom near Lydda (Diospolis in Palestine) before the time of the Emperor Constantine. It is possible that he was a soldier. By the sixth century St George had become a popular saint. Plentiful legends about him survive in Greek, Latin, Armenian, Coptic, Syriac, Ethiopian and Turkish.

No one is quite certain how St George came to be the patron saint of England. The cult of George flourished in England during the Crusades. George personified the ideal of Christian chivalry and became the patron saint of soldiers. Richard I placed himself and his army under the saint's protection. Under Edward III George became patron of the Order of the Garter; at the battle of Agincourt Henry V (in Shakespeare, at any rate) invoked him as England's patron.

St George's dragon first appears in the twelfth century and is recounted in the thirteenth century *Golden Legend*, a manual of the lives of the saints, which was translated and printed by Caxton. The dragon was a local pest that terrorized the whole country. Its breath was said to poison all who approached it. It fed on a diet of two sheep a day: when there were no more sheep in the country, human victims were offered instead. One day the lot fell on the king's daughter. She went to the dragon to meet her fate dressed as a bride. At this point St George appeared. Single-handedly he attacked the beast and pierced it with his sword. He then made a lead from the princess' girdle and led the dragon through the town for all to see. St George reassured the townsfolk by saying that he would kill the dragon if all the town were baptised. The king and all his subjects agreed. Fifteen thousand people were baptised and the dragon was slain.

St George and his dragon might not have the best historical credentials but it is a good story with a clear message of good triumphing over evil.

Dragons are still popular mythical beasts. Most children have a clear idea about what they look like. The dragon in the story of St George is a symbol of evil, of all that makes us fearful or frightened. St George shows how God's people can successfully fight evil and overcome it in Christ's name. In Christian art St George's shield, emblazoned with the St George's cross, serves as a visual reminder of this.

Before starting these activities discuss with the children what frightens them.

FOR YOUNGER CHILDREN

A St George and dragon collage

Ask one child to lie down on a large sheet of thick paper or card and get the other children to draw around him. Cut out the outline. This card model can be made into a St George. His armour can be made from glueing bottle tops or small foil pie dishes to the outline. Use a rubber-based glue. The children can then draw in the other features and shield.

Before the class, draw an outline of a dragon on a large sheet of paper. After the children

have discussed the things which frighten them they can then write or draw these things on pieces of paper. The pieces of paper can then be stuck on to the dragon.

FOR OLDER CHILDREN

Modern dragons

Continue the discussion with the older children about the things which frighten them. You can also discuss what are modern 'dragons' or evils which threaten the community. This might lead to a discussion on the environment, war or poverty. Ask the children to draw a large outline of the dragon illustrated. They can then take it turns to write about modern 'dragons' in the dragon, writing around its shape as shown in the diagram. They should use different colours so that the whole dragon is full of the 'modern' dragons of our society. This could lead on to a discussion about how Christians can 'fight' these modern 'dragons'.

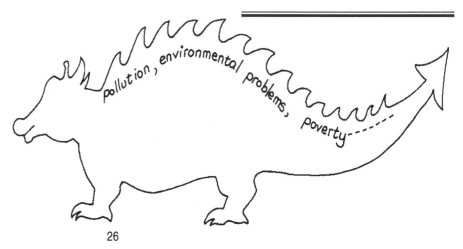

How Mark Brought the Good News

First the news headlines – the direct style of broadcasters today had its biblical equivalent in the Gospel according to St Mark: 'The beginning of the gospel of Jesus Christ the Son of God' sets the breathless pace of the action. The identity of the evangelist has not been established for certain, but he is usually identified with the John Mark of Acts whose mother's house in Jerusalem was a meeting place for the apostles. Some maintain he was the young man who followed Christ after his arrest and then escaped capture in Gethsemane (Mark 14.51).

John Mark is a central character in the biblical accounts of the early Church. He is a companion of Paul, Peter and the cousin of St Barnabas (Col. 4.10). He travels with Paul and Barnabas on the first missionary journey (Acts 12.12,25; 13.5,13; 15.37-39), but after an argument, Mark turns back at Perga to go to Jerusalem. He later preaches with Barnabas in Cyprus (Acts 15.39). Paul refers to Mark when he is imprisoned in Rome (Col. 4.10, Philem. 24, 2 Tim. 4.11,). Peter refers to him as his 'son' (1 Pet. 5.13) and he is with Peter in Rome. Traditionally the Gospel of Mark was believed to represent the teachings and memoirs of Peter.

clothed in bishop's robes as tradition maintains he was bishop of Alexandria. Children can be encouraged to illuminate the letter 'M' with symbols that illustrate St Mark's life and include his emblem. See the templates. They might also illuminate the first letter of their own name with symbols that illustrate their own life.

FOR OLDER CHILDREN
Telling the story today

Discuss with the children ways we have for communicating news today – newspapers, radio, books, film, drama, television, etc.

Divide the children into two groups. Ask the first group to prepare a short mime of one episode in St Mark's life. The second group should watch the mime and think how they would prepare a radio commentary for the

Presenting the Good News

'Go out to the whole world, and preach the gospel to all creatures' (Mark 16.15). (Introductory sentence for St Mark's Day in the ASB).

When St Mark wrote his Gospel, written communication was in the form of papyrus scrolls. Today we communicate our news in very different ways. The aim of these activity suggestions is to get children to consider the different ways of communicating good news and to learn more about the life of St Mark.

The scroll story

You will need a roll of paper, pencils, felt-tip pens, a New Testament.

The biblical references in the introductory text can be used as the basis for scenes in St Mark's life. Divide the children into groups and give each group one episode in St Mark's life to read about and discuss: in Gethsemane with Christ, on the first missionary journey with Paul, preaching with Barnabas, with Peter in Rome, etc. Then unroll the paper and ask each group to write down and illustrate the episodes to form a scroll story of St Mark's life.

The illuminated text

In later church history the Bible and religious books were richly illuminated. The decoration of the text was in itself an act of devotion.

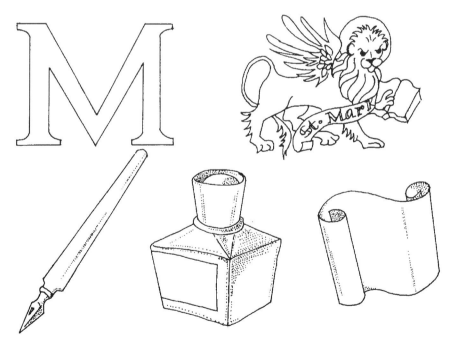

These illuminated manuscripts would often emphasise the first letter or the first line of a chapter. An example of this is the Lindisfarne Gospels which are housed in the British Museum. These were written and decorated at the end of the seventh century and provide one of the finest surviving examples of early Hiberno-Saxon art. Illuminated manuscripts would often incorporate symbols and intricate geometric patterns. The emblem of St Mark is a lion. Paintings of him may also include a pen, ink and a scroll. He is often shown

episode. Ask the mime group to repeat their performance with one person from the radio group giving a commentary. Now ask the radio reporters to act out another incident from St Mark's life while the second group watch and work out a television news commentary for the episode. Discuss with the groups the advantages and disadvantages of different forms of communication.

Philip and James – The May Day Apostles

Most of what we know about St Philip and St James is from the New Testament. Philip appears in the Gospels and the Acts of the Apostles. From John 1.43-52, we learn that he is from Bethsaida in Galilee. He heard Jesus's call and then encouraged Nathanael to 'come and see' Jesus. He was present at the feeding of the five thousand, commenting that 200 pennyworth of bread was not enough to feed the crowd (John 6.7).

At the last supper Philip asks Jesus to show them the Father. Jesus replies 'Have I been with you so long, and yet you do not know me, Philip? He who has seen me has seen the Father . . . Believe me that I am in the Father and the Father in me.' (RSV: see John 14.1-14). Philip is in the upper room at Pentecost (Acts 1. 12-14), and then disappears from the New Testament text. Polycrates of Ephesus says that he died of natural causes at Hierapolis, and links him with Asia; but other traditions maintain he was crucified.

There are so many Jameses in the New Testament that it is easy to get confused. The James who is remembered on 1 May is James the Less (as distinct from James the Great, the son of Zebedee, traditionally linked with Santiago de Compostela). James the Less is appropriately named. We know less about him than about most of the apostles. He is thought to have been James the son of Alphaeus in Mark 3.18. He has been identified with the James whose mother stood by Christ on the cross (Mark 15.40). James, the Lord's brother, is thought to be a different James.

Philip's ministry

Philip was a questioning disciple, well-meaning but shown as one who had not quite understood Jesus' greatness. The story of Philip provides a useful starting-point for a discussion on ministry. He was a disciple, an apostle and a missionary. His come-and-see type of evangelism brought Nathanael to Jesus.

A ministry frieze

Discuss with the group who brought them to church, or who helped them understand more about Jesus? You can then discuss the different ways in which people have come to be in the group.

To illustrate the discussion you can make a link-person frieze. Give each child the paper outlines of two people holding hands. You can make a large paper-dolly chain to do this, and cut them into twos. The children should draw themselves on one of the outlines, and on the other outline a picture of the person who most influenced them. The pictures can be mounted on a large sheet of paper with all the people linking hands (see diagram). The group can then think of a heading for the frieze and draw in a suitable background.

James the Less

With James the Less there is more of a problem. We know so little about him that there are few stories to tell children. One way to remember him is to look at the idea of 'less' or 'younger'. Younger people in the church often seem to have less importance than adults. What they have to say may be seen as of less value. Jesus showed that everyone was of equal worth; no one was disregarded. Young people or small things are often important. Although we know little about James the Less, he was chosen by Jesus as one of his disciples. Discuss with the children how small things are often essential: an apple pip makes a tree, a match flame becomes a large fire, drops of rain a large puddle, and so on. This could provide an opportunity for collecting different vegetable and fruit seeds, planting and growing them. The children can then compare the size of seed with the plant two months later.

Apostles

Philip and James were both apostles: people sent by God to pass on the good news. Discuss with the group the various different ways of communication: one-to-one discussion, a teacher to a class, radio, television, telephone, fax, photographs, paintings, television, video and so on.

Then tell them the story of the feeding of the five thousand. Ask them to shut their eyes and imagine that they took part in the feeding and listened to Jesus. Then ask them to think of the best way to communicate their experience to a friend they see every day and to a pen-friend who they don't know very well. Discuss with them what might be the best type of communication in each case. They can then retell their story in the ways they have chosen.

A Saint for Modern Times

JULIAN OF NORWICH

8 MAY

Julian of Norwich told her readers to forget her and to look to Jesus. Her writings – *Revelations of Divine Love* – are a spiritual classic. But today readers and scholars alike are curious to find out more about this fourteenth-century woman who speaks so directly to modern Christians.

Apart from a handful of references after her death most of what we know about Julian of Norwich comes from her own writings. Julian herself tells us that she received her revelations from God on 8 May 1373 when she was 30 and at the point of death. She lived in a cell by a church; it is likely that she took her name from the church's dedication.

Anchorites and anchoresses were common in the Middle Ages. It is unclear whether Julian became an anchoress before or after her religious experience. Her knowledge and sympathy for the care a mother gives a child has led many to suppose that she was a widow. Others presume she was a Benedictine nun from Carrow Abbey.

Julian says that she is 'unlettered' and this has given rise to much debate by modern scholars. Her writings are not only a unique spiritual work but the earliest known writings in English by a woman.

Julian's influence has been widespread in the twentieth century from the small Julian prayer cells to those who champion her as the first feminist theologian. Her writings contain many images which resonate today. Throughout the Revelations the cross is the central image she uses to show God's love for humankind. Julian was certain, despite the terrible times she lived in, that God was in control. 'All shall be well, and all manner of thing shall be well.' Julian uses many images to underline the wonder of this love, the most notable of which is her image of God as Mother.

There is a wealth of published material and resources on Julian. In Norwich the Julian Centre and her Church are open every day.

More than 600 years separate children from Julian of Norwich: it is not easy to make her accessible to them. Julian's life was dedicated to prayer. Teachers might want to focus on different prayer aids, or discuss the religious life with children. Another way to make her come alive is to use some of her better-known sayings as a basis for activities.

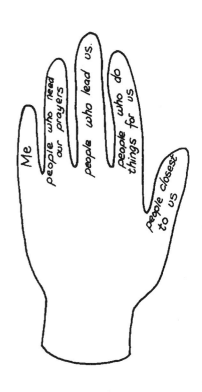

As small as a hazelnut

In her Revelations Julian is shown a little thing by the Lord, the size of a hazelnut in the palm of her hand. 'In this little thing she saw three truths: The first is that God made it; the second is that God loves it; and the third is that God looks after it.'

Give each child a hazelnut. Ask them to look at it carefully and then discuss the following questions with them:

● Why is the hazelnut so well made?

● How does God love it and look after it?

After the discussion, ask the children to take the hazelnut home and put it in the pocket of their coat. Every time they feel the hazelnut in the bottom of their pocket they can be reminded that God loves everything no matter how small.

Another idea on this theme is give each child a small matchbox the week before the class. Ask them to fill the matchbox with as many different small things from nature as possible. During the class, these objects can be the subject of a discussion as above.

A prayer hand

Variants on the idea of a prayer hand are popular with children. Give younger children a large cut-out cardboard hand. Older children can draw around one of their own hands and cut out the outline. On the hand they should write:

● Thumb – people closest to us (the nearest digit, so for those nearest).

● Index finger – people who help us (the strong finger for doctors, nurses, teachers).

● The tallest finger – people who lead us.

● The ring finger – people in need (a symbol of love, this finger to remind the children of all those they love who need their prayers).

● The little finger – me.

The prayer hand helps children remember who to pray for. They can write the Lord's prayer on the back of the hand and take it home to put up as a reminder.

Alternatively teachers might want to use the idea of an intercessions box. The children can make their own boxes and put in prayer reminders during the week.

Training to be a Team Leader

'And they cast lots for them, and the lot fell on Matthias; and he was enrolled with the eleven apostles.' (Acts 1.26, RSV)

Matthias was not one of the original band of 12 disciples, but after Judas' betrayal another apostle had to be found. The essential qualifications of an apostle were to have been a follower of Christ and a witness of the resurrection. Acts 1. 15-26 records that there were two candidates, Joseph Barsabbas and Matthias. Lots were cast and Matthias was chosen.

Matthias is one of the great unknowns. A faithful disciple and apostle who was present at the first Pentecost but who then disappears from the New Testament record.

In celebrating the feast of St Matthias on 14 May the children's worker is presented with a challenge – we know so little about him. Like many followers of Christ, he was not famous. But saints, according to St Paul are all the faithful members of the Christian community, the famous and the unknown. The Feast of St Matthias is therefore an appropriate time to remember all those unsung faithful followers of Christ.

Discussion

Discuss with the group how a football team is run, with some merely 'in the squad' and others among the chosen players. Have they ever had to sit through a match and then be called upon to play at the last minute? What did it feel like?

Explain that Matthias' calling was unexpected. Judas had betrayed Jesus and so another apostle had to be found to make the group complete. You could use the image of a sports team as an example of how all Christians have to 'train and be ready', but not all are called upon to play a public part and be a star.

Making the team complete

After the resurrection the disciples needed to find a substitute for Judas. This image of an incomplete 'team' can be made visual in a game.

In advance of the session the leader needs to draw a large circle on a sheet of card (about the size of a washing up bowl). Draw a second circle within this. Then fold the circle into 12. Cut out the 12 outer segments of the circle. Write the names of the 12 disciples on each of these 12 segments. Cut each segment in half, breaking the names in two. Draw a picture of Jesus at the Last Supper in the remaining circle.

Repeat the process with a second sheet of card, leaving the centre of the circle bare. On the segments of these circles write the names of the 12 apostles, including Matthias.

The leader should keep the Matthias segment, and hide the remaining 46 bits of paper around the room before the group enter. Then tell them that they have to find the 12 disciples to sit with Jesus at the Last Supper. They then have to find the 12 apostles to put around the second circle or table. Who is missing from the second table?

Why is the circle incomplete? The leader should then produce Matthias's name.

The apostle's lot

Write the names of different types of job on slips of paper. Make sure there is a slip of paper for each member of the group. Include a wide variety of jobs: a clown, a bus conductor, an opera singer and a gardener. Make sure an apostle is included.

Next ask every child to pick a slip of paper from a hat. Each child in turn then has to mime their job. The other children have to guess the occupation of the person doing the mime by asking five questions. The person miming may only nod or shake their head in reply. It might take them some time to guess the occupation of the apostle but the game will remind the group how Matthias was chosen and the work that he did.

A saints board

Discuss with the group who are the saints, the special people who have helped them know about Jesus.

Can they think of saints who might not be well-known but whose lives and work are examples of Christian love and service?

Can they think of saints in their own church and community whose faithful work goes unnoticed?

Take two large sheets of card to the group. Stick them together with sticky tape. On top of the card write `the saints of . . . ' and then the name of the church. Ask one group of children to draw pictures of all those saints in history who have been an example to them. On the second side of the board another group should draw pictures of all those in their own church community who are an example of the Christian life.

FOR YOUNGER CHILDREN
Thank you badges

Ask the children to make a 'thank you' badge with a smiling face to give to a 'saint' in their own church or community. See the illustration.

The Father of English History

Contrary to *1066 and All That*, Bede was neither Venomous, nor was he the author of *The Rosary*. He acquired the title 'Venerable' in the ninth century, in recognition of his holy life and of his singular importance to the English Church. He it was who first described its origins and development and chronicled its saints and sinners. Without Bede's *A History of the English Church and People* the wealth of stories about how the Christian gospel came to these islands would have been lost.

Bede was born near Sunderland in 673 and educated from the age of seven, first by Benedict Biscop at Wearmouth and then by Ceolfrith at Jarrow. He never travelled far from the monastery at Jarrow where he spent the rest of his life. He was ordained deacon in about 692 and priested when he was about 30. Within his lifetime Bede was renowned as a scholar and said of himself that his 'special delight was always to learn, to teach, and to write'.

Bede's life was uneventful, but his writing had an enormous influence on the church of his day and after. He wrote works on orthography, metre, chronology, poetry, the lives of the saints, of abbots and many biblical commentaries. The History was completed in 731. It is in this volume of books that we learn of the great people of the early English Church, from Alban to Wilfrid; of the Synod of Whitby and the growing influence of the Roman ecclesiastical system. On the 1200th anniversary of Bede's death Bishop Hensley Henson of Durham wrote: 'The more closely Bede's career is studied, the more amazing it appears. In him two streams of spiritual influence seemed to meet and blend – the evangelistic passion of the Celtic missionaries, and the disciplined devotion of the Benedictine monks.'

Until his death Bede worked on his writings. According to an account by one of his scholars, Cuthbert, Bede spent his last days singing the psalms and dictating. He died on 25 May 735.

Bede's ecclesiastical history became widely known on the Continent and in England. Within 50 years of his death his cult as a saint was established. His relics have been in Durham Cathedral since the mid eleventh century.

Schools and church groups interested in learning more about Bede can visit Jarrow Hall to see a permanent exhibition on the life and times of Bede.

Europe's oldest coloured window, now in St Paul's, Jarrow, came from the monastery refectory there.

From his writings Bede gives clear information about the daily life of a monk. Each monk was given tasks according to his abilities whether in the garden, the kitchen or writing, copying and illuminating manuscripts. The day's worship began with matins and lauds in the early hours and ended with compline at the end of the day. Describe the life of a monk to the group.

FOR YOUNGER CHILDREN
An illuminated manuscript

Many monasteries at the time of Bede produced magnificent illuminated manuscripts of the scriptures. The monk's life was directed

to God's service; his art was to give God glory. Discuss with the group what are the three most important things in each child's life. It might be parents, friends, pets or toys.

Ask them to draw the initial letter of each thing and decorate these letters as beautifully as they can.

FOR OLDER CHILDREN
Priorities in life

Ask the group to think of two or three activities, people or things which they regard as the most important to their lives. It might be a friend, sport, pets, study, prayer, parents, a musical instrument, etc. Ask them to plan a timetable for three days in which these important activities, people or things receive their best attention.

The monks at Jarrow gave their best attention to the work which they believed God wanted them to do. They therefore divided their day between worship, work and service.

FOR ALL AGES
A stained-glass window

Jarrow is famous for its stained glass. Those who made it wanted to show something of God's glory. Ask the children to design a small round stained glass window which uses colour, shape or a drawing to show something of God's goodness.

There are a number of different ways of making a window: You can use greaseproof paper and felt-tip pens, making the window tracery with a black one. Or you can make the tracery from black sugar paper, and on the reverse stick coloured tissue or cellophane paper.

From Rome to Canterbury

The story goes that one day in Rome Gregory, who was to become Pope, noticed some fair-skinned people. He asked who they were and was told they were Angles. He commented 'non Angli, sed Angeli' not Angles but angels. Many years later Pope Gregory was to send his envoy, Augustine, to Britain to evangelise the Anglo-Saxons.

St Augustine of Canterbury was Italian by birth. He was a monk and prior of St Andrew on the Coelian Hill in Rome, before Pope Gregory chose him for his new mission. Augustine and his party of 40 monks did not share Gregory's enthusiasm for the angels of Britain. In Gaul the party got cold feet: 'They became afraid, and began to consider returning home. For they were appalled at the idea of going to a barbarous, fierce and pagan nation' (Bede). Pope Gregory urged them to continue and arranged for Augustine to be consecrated bishop.

Kent was not as barbaric as the party had anticipated. They landed at Ebbsfleet in 597 and were received by Ethelbert, King of Kent. Ethelbert gave them accommodation in Canterbury; and from here Augustine and his fellow missionaries preached the gospel. The King became so impressed with the sincerity of Augustine and his men and the miracles that they performed, that he was baptised. Thousands of his subjects followed him.

Augustine constantly referred to Pope Gregory for advice. Thirty of the letters from Gregory about his mission to Britain survive. In 601 Gregory sent Augustine several colleagues and clergy. Gregory also sent Augustine the pallium (a circular band of white woollen material and marked with six dark purple crosses which was given to archbishops) and gave him practical instructions for the appointments of bishops in Britain. A cathedral was built at Canterbury. Augustine, as the first Archbishop of Canterbury, was successful in establishing a basic ecclesiastical structure in the country. He was less successful in working with the existing Celtic church which survived in Britain.

Ask the group whether they think the church always makes people welcome. How did they feel when they first came to church? What were they expecting? What did they find? Discuss with the group how they think their church could make people more welcome.

To illustrate the discussion, draw a large picture of your church on card. On the roof of the church write the word WELCOME. Give each child a sheet of paper and ask them to draw an outline of a person. On that person they should write or draw a picture of the ways they can help make people feel more welcome. Stick the completed figures around the card church and display.

The bishop's badges

On a different theme, St Augustine's day on 26 May may provide an opportunity for discussion about bishops. Many children will have the opportunity to see a bishop in May and June during confirmations and ordinations. The symbolism of the bishop's insignia or badges is not immediately apparent to children but by explaining their significance children can understand more about the office of bishop. The group could make models of the insignia.

● A bishop's ring is usually set with an amethyst. Just as a wedding ring symbolises the love and faithfulness between a husband and wife the bishop's ring symbolises the bishop's faithfulness to the Church.

● A mitre is the liturgical head-dress of a bishop. The tongue shape of a mitre is a reminder of the tongues of fire which lit on the apostles at the first Pentecost.

● The pastoral staff or crosier is modelled on the crook-shaped staff of shepherds. The bishop's crosier reminds people that the bishop is earthly representative of the chief shepherd of the people.

● The pectoral cross, which is often made from precious metal, shows the badge of all Christians.

FOR ALL AGES
A church reaching out

St Augustine and his 40 monks used their base in Canterbury to reach out to people from all walks of life. They preached the gospel and showed the love of God in practical ways. This activity can form part of a parish day and provides a visual reminder that the church is for everyone.

Draw a large outline of your church on a piece of card. Over the outline draw jigsaw pieces. Display the church jigsaw. Ask everyone in the group to cut out a piece of the jigsaw and write on this the groups of people who they think the church should be reaching out to.

Ask the group to return their pieces to the jigsaw and then discuss practical ways of reaching out to the wider community.

FOR OLDER CHILDREN
A welcoming church

Ask a child to read out the story of the call of the disciples (Mark 1.16-19) and discuss how Jesus encouraged people to follow him.

Signs of the Holy Spirit

The book of Acts uses powerful, dynamic language – noise, wind, fire – to describe the coming of the Holy Spirit at the first Pentecost (Acts 2.1-4). Elsewhere in the Bible, the Holy Spirit is portrayed as a dove. These images provide an excellent starting point for an exploration with children of the meaning of the Holy Spirit.

Fire

Fire is used in other parts of the Bible to illustrate God's presence. Read the story of Moses and the burning bush to the children from Exodus 3. Then read Exodus 13.21-22, which tells how God led the Israelites from Egypt.

Get the children to consider where fire is used in church: the Paschal candle, altar candles, baptism candles and sanctuary lamps.

Wind

Using wind as an image of the power of God is not confined to the New Testament. The common Hebrew word for wind is rûah, which can be translated 'spirit' or 'breath' depending on its context. In the Exodus story God is shown to have power over wind (Exodus 10.13,19). He is also in the breath of life, (Psalm 104. 29-30). Early Christian writers referred to the Holy Spirit as the energy of God. Read John 3.8 aloud from a children's Bible and ask the group what the writer means.

In a group, get the children to describe what wind is. Practise making the different sounds wind makes: a gentle wind, a hurricane and a storm. Get the group to consider the many uses of wind as a source of power. Explain to the children that we cannot see wind but we can see its powerful effects. The Holy Spirit is invisible, but its work can be seen.

Doves

Although a dove does not appear in the Pentecost narrative, it is a good symbol of the Holy Spirit to use with children. Ask them what a dove reminds them of and what are its characteristics.

Remind the children of the Genesis story of Noah, who sends a dove to see if the floods had gone down (Genesis 8.6-12). Get the children to read Matthew 3.16, when John baptises Jesus. Then ask them what message God gives through a dove at the baptism of Jesus.

These activities aim to help the children understand something of the excitement of the first Pentecost.

FOR OLDER CHILDREN
A dove kite

You will need A3 or A4 paper taped together, straws, glue, staples, a hole-puncher, a tail 2cm x 4m long and a kite line or thin string.

Method (the numbers on figures 1 and 2 refer to the instruction numbers):

1 Fold the sheet of paper in half and copy figure 1 onto it. (Several copies could be made beforehand and given to the children.)

2 Cut out around the outline.

3 Open the paper out and place a short straw inside the body along the front fold. Then staple or stick together to the dotted line.

4 Staple the ends of a drinking straw to the top of each wing. The straw should hold the wings back.

5 Staple on a tail 2cm x 4m long. This can be made from paper, streamers, plastic strips from bin-liners, etc.

6 Punch a hole for the kite line through the body. Thin string, garden twine or even button thread can be used.

On Whitsunday afternoon the children can fly their doves and feel the power of the wind pulling the kite.

FOR ALL AGES
A wind garden

In Acts the Holy Spirit is described as a noise that is like a strong driving wind. This wind garden helps children visualise the powerful effect of wind.

You will need a garden tray or polystyrene packaging, twigs, cocktail sticks, milk-bottle tops, buttons, strips of paper, foil strips from pie dishes, sweet wrappers, fine string or wool, tissue paper, sticky tape, a hair-dryer or fan.

The numbers in figure 3 refer to the instruction numbers):

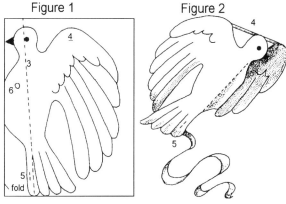
Figure 1

Figure 2

1 The garden can be made by planting items into soil in a polystyrene container. Make the tree by planting small branches or twigs. Tie any of the items to lengths of wool or string and hang them from the branches so that they hit one another to make a noise when the wind blows.

2 Small tissue-paper streamers can be attached to the branches.

3 Flowers can be made by cutting a fringe into a strip of tissue paper and winding the uncut end around a cocktail stick which is then stuck into the ground.

4 Other flowers can be made from sweet wrappers attached to cocktail sticks.

5 Real turf or moss can cover the soil. Alternatively, double-sided sticky tape can stick fringes of green tissue paper on a polystyrene base.

An adult should then place the garden by a fan or hair dryer and show the group the effect of 'wind' on it.

Figure 3

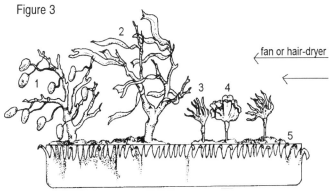

Trinity Sunday

Trinity Sunday is often ignored by those who work with children; and yet the three-fold invocation of Father, Son and Holy Spirit is frequently used in worship and is well within the experience of many children. So too is the idea of 'three in one' familiar to those members of the Scout or Guide Movement: they know the three-fold promise.

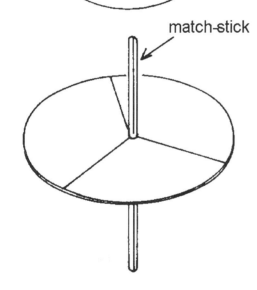

match-stick

FOR YOUNGER CHILDREN

A Trinity spinning top

The three parts of the spinning top look as though they are all one when the top is spun.

You will need thick cardboard, scissors, pens or crayons, used matches, and something about 10cm in diameter to draw round.

Method: draw a circle about 10cm in diameter on the cardboard and cut it out. Mark the centre of the circle, and then draw lines to the middle to give three equal parts. The words 'Father', 'Son', and 'Holy Spirit' can be written one on each section (or if preferred three

symbols of hand raised in blessing, cross and tongues of fire can be drawn instead). The circle can be coloured as required.

Make a small hole through the centre point of the circle. Push the used match-stick gently through the hole until it is about half-way through. The top will now spin and the three sections will look like one.

FOR OLDER CHILDREN

A HOLY, HOLY, HOLY banner

This idea is based on the ASB Old Testament reading, Isaiah 6. 1-8. Discuss with the children ways to describe the glory of God. In Christian tradition, 'Holy, holy, holy' has come to describe God, Father, Son and Holy Spirit.

You will need a large sheet of paper (A1 size) in any colour, pieces of white paper about 10cm square, scissors, glue, felt-tip pens, two bean canes (one about 90cm and the other about 60cm long), a short length of wool or garden twine, sticky tape or masking tape, and examples of illuminated letters from manuscripts.

Draw one letter of the words HOLY, HOLY, HOLY on each of the pieces of white paper. Show examples of decorated letters. Each child then takes a letter and decorates it in bright patterns; as much of the white background as poss-ible should be covered.

Trim the letters so that no white surround shows, and glue them on to the large coloured paper to form the words HOLY, HOLY, HOLY. Add a decorated border.

To make the banner, bind the two bean canes together with twine or wool to form a cross: see diagram. Using masking tape or sticky tape, hang the A1 paper from the horizontal cane.

If there are enough children, the banner can be double-sided. The children should be given the chance to carry it at a suitable event.

Three ways of looking at me

For children who enjoy writing (or tape-recording).

You will need pencils, paper, rubber, and a cassette recorder and blank tape if they are to record.

Ask each child to write a paragraph (or speak for a short while) about themselves – how they like others to regard them.

Then they pretend they are their five-year-old brother and then their teacher at school and write a record how they imagine the small brother and the teacher regard them. These can be read (or played back) to all the group.

How many people are you describing? ONE. How many aspects of that person are you describing? THREE.

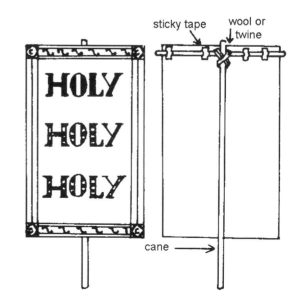

A Saint for Europe

The story of Boniface is the story of a remarkable English monk, preacher, missionary, archbishop and statesman who had a profound effect on the organisation of a united Christian Europe half a century before the reign of Charlemagne.

The first life of Boniface was written about ten years after his death by a monk named Willibald. Many letters written by Boniface also survive. Boniface (meaning doer of good deeds), originally known as Winfrith (meaning friend of peace), was born to land-owning Anglo-Saxon peasants in Crediton, Devon, in about AD 680. He was educated in monasteries in Exeter and at the Benedictine house at Nursling, near Winchester. Boniface was ordained at 30 and in 716 he left England to follow the work of Wilfrid and Willibrord as a missionary in Frisia (northern Holland).

German bishop

Pope Gregory II asked Boniface to be a missionary in Germany in Bavaria and Thuringia. In 722 the Pope made Boniface bishop of all Germany east of Rhine. On his return to Hesse from Rome, Boniface found many new converts had returned to their pagan ways. He decided to strike at the heart of the pagan beliefs. He summoned people to the giant oak of Geismar, a sacred tree dedicated to Thor, and centre of the cult of the thunder-god in Germany. Once a crowd had assembled Boniface took an axe and started to cut the tree down. Willibald records that as soon as Boniface had made a V-shaped cut, a great wind dashed the old trunk to the ground and split it into the shape of a cross. The people, amazed that Thor did not punish Boniface, became Christians. Boniface used the timber from the fallen oak to build a simple chapel. A later German legend says that a tiny fir tree sprang up among the roots of Thor's Oak, and this was the first Christmas tree.

Boniface knew how to make friends. His ability to evangelise in wide areas of Europe was helped by papal support and co-operation from the local rulers and counts. He was made archbishop by Pope Gregory III in 732 and given permission to consecrate new bishops.

Reforming the Church of the Franks

In 741 Charles Martel, ruler of the Franks, died and his sons divided his lands. Boniface worked through the two brothers to improve church discipline. Between 742 and 747 he presided over a series of reforming councils. Abuses in the church were condemned. The Rule of St Benedict was made the basic code for all Carolingian monasteries. In 751 Boniface crowned Martel's son, Pepin, King of the Franks at Soissons and anointed him with chrism, so securing the alliance between the Franks and the Papacy.

Martyrdom in Frisia

Despite his fame and his success in uniting many of the churches in Europe, at the end of his life Archbishop Boniface returned to Frisia. Here he met his martyrdom from a group of pagans on 5 June in 754 or 755. Boniface's body was returned to Fulda and his tomb became a place of pilgrimage.

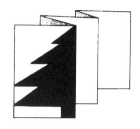

showing how they could live up to these names in their own lives. Older children might consider which well-known present-day people could be called a friend of peace or doer of good deeds.

FOR OLDER CHILDREN

The life of St Boniface can provide an excellent starting-point for older children to learn more about the history and geography of eighth-century Europe. These activities are designed so that few books and resources are needed but teachers can easily augment the material for further exploration.

You will need enlarged photocopies of the map illustrated, an atlas, drawing and painting implements, paper, scissors, cardboard boxes, glue and lolly sticks.

The journeys of St Boniface

Using the map as a basis ask the children to follow the footsteps of St Boniface through-out Europe. They can be given an atlas of Europe and encouraged to trace the routes themselves. They can then draw a large map of Europe marking all the places which are important in Boniface's life. At each of the locations ask them to draw a simple picture of what happened.

Building up a church

Boniface helped build many simple wooden churches in Germany. Older children might like to build simple models using cardboard boxes or wooden lolly sticks.

FOR YOUNGER CHILDREN

For both activities you will need paper, card, drawing implements, scissors, collage materials.

A fir tree story

Get the children to fold a long sheet of paper backwards and forwards in accordion folds as shown in the diagram. Copy the template illustrated and draw an outline of half a fir tree. Make sure that at least some of the branches touch the fold. Carefully cut through all the layers of paper and cut round the tree shape. When the paper is unfolded the children can use each tree to illustrate one incident in the life of St Boniface.

A name collage

Boniface had two names, each with a special meaning. Ask the children to make a collage

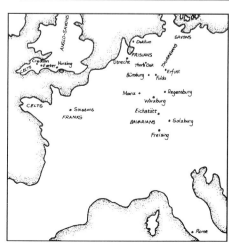

Welcome the Pilgrims

A *thin place,* said George MacLeod of Iona, *only a tissue paper separating the material from the spiritual.* Over the centuries thousands of pilgrims have crossed the seas to this rocky island in the Hebrides. Once a burial ground for Scottish kings, Iona has provided material for writers, poets and bards. The first was Columba.

St Columba came from a noble Irish family in Donegal: he was born around AD 521. He was trained in Irish monasteries, including Clonard, where St Finnian was abbot. Columba went on to found several monasteries himself, among them Derry, Durrow and probably Kells.

About 563 he left Ireland with 12 companions and went to Iona and set up a monastery. Here he lived for 34 years, evangelising the islands and mainland. He is said to have converted Brude, King of the Picts, and in 574 the Irish King, Aidan of Dalriada, was consecrated by him. As Abbot of Iona, Columba was the chief ecclesiastical power in the whole region.

Columba's life is mentioned in Bede's ecclesiastical history. He says of Columba: 'Whatever type of man he may have been, we know for certain that he left successors distinguished for their purity of life, their love of God, and their loyalty to the monastic rule.' A fuller life was written by Adamnan, who was also an Abbot of Iona and lived from about 625 to 704. From

Adamnan we hear of Columba as saint, visionary, prophet and miracle-worker. He was scholar, poet and ruler with a fearless commitment to God. Three surviving Latin poems are ascribed to him; his skills as a scribe can be seen in the Cathach of Columba, a late sixth-century psalter in the Irish Academy.

Iona became a centre for missionary activity both in Scotland and beyond until Viking raids in the ninth century, when most of the monks moved to Ireland. In 1203 the Benedictines rebuilt the Abbey and settled as a community. There was also a medieval nunnery on Iona. After the Reformation the Abbey fell into ruins. It was not until this century that Iona once again became a centre of pilgrimage.

The modern Iona Community was established by Dr George Fielden MacLeod. Dr MacLeod worked as a Scottish Presbyterian minister in Govan, Glasgow. He saw the enormous difficulties the churches had in communicating with ordinary working and unemployed people. To address this problem he set out to rebuild the ruined Iona Abbey, using the skills of unemployed masons and carpenters. He arranged that trainee ministers worked as their labourers. The clergy were also trained to work in the slums and housing schemes of Scotland. The training scheme for Presbyterian ministers developed into an ecumenical community of men and women, ordained and lay. The Very Revd Lord MacLeod of Fuinary died in 1991. The community that was once denounced as being 'half-way towards Rome and half-way towards Moscow' has grown: it now has 200 members. Members are united by a discipline of prayer, sharing of time and finances and meeting together to work for justice and peace.

Hospitality in church

Visitors have always made their way to Iona. The first monks were renowned for their hospitality. This activity helps children practise the same gift in their own church.

First discuss with the group what Jesus said about welcoming strangers, (Matt. 25.35). Then ask them what the journey to Iona must have been like, and how special the welcome must have been to the visitors. Iona was a place of hospitality for travellers, pilgrims and those who came seeking advice. The children could welcome the rest of the congregation by making shortbread or oatmeal biscuits in Sunday school and serving them with coffee after the service.

A prayer hut

Talk with the group about times when they want to hide away: where do they go and what do they do? Explain that Jesus sometimes decided to be alone with his Father (Mark 1.35), and that time apart with God can help them, too.

The monks of Iona would have lived in individual beehive cells made from mud and wattle.

The group can build their own prayer hut by using chairs and blankets. Put a cushion, Bible and a torch in the hut. The children can then take it in turns to spend a few minutes quietly in the hut (use an egg-timer). The rest of the group can write out and decorate copies of this prayer of the Iona Community. The prayer can then be used in quiet times at home.

Deep peace of the running wave to you.
Deep peace of the flowing air to you.
Deep peace of the quiet earth to you.
Deep peace of the shining stars to you.
Deep peace of the Son of Peace to you.
Amen.

Britain's First Christian Martyr

S t Alban was Britain's first martyr, and the town named after him is Britain's oldest pilgrimage centre. According to Bede and other biographers, Alban was a pagan of Verulamium, the Latin name for St Albans.

One day he gave shelter to a priest, traditionally known as Amphibalus, who was fleeing from persecutors. Alban was so impressed by what the priest told him that he became a Christian. The Emperor sent soldiers to find the priest but Alban took the priest's cloak from him and was arrested instead. The judge was angry when he realised that they had arrested the wrong man. He ordered Alban to offer sacrifices to pagan gods. Alban refused and when the judge asked him his name, he replied: 'My parents named me Alban, and I worship and adore the living, the true God, who created all things.' Alban was condemned to be flogged in an attempt to change his belief. According to Bede, Alban suffered great torture but did not renounce his faith. He was then ordered to be beheaded. The judge's plans were further frustrated when the executioner became a convert and another had to be found.

Bede records a number of miracles at the time of Alban's execution on 22 June. Alban asked God to give him water and immediately a stream bubbled up at his feet. The first executioner was killed with Alban. Bede tells us that as Alban was beheaded the eyes of the second executioner dropped out. The judge was so impressed with these strange miracles he called a halt to the persecution. Scholars debate the time of his martyrdom. It used to be connected with the persecution under Diocletian (c 305), but most now believe it to have been under Decius (c 254) or Septimius Severus (c 209).

Drama

The story of St Alban's conversion and martyrdom provides exciting material for a play.

You will need at least five characters: Alban, the priest, the judge, the two executioners, and a crowd. Children can take it in turns to play the different parts.

Pilgrimage through the ages

Since St Albans is the oldest centre for pilgrimage in Britain, you could discuss with the group how people travelled to holy places on pilgrimages. With older groups you could read parts of Chaucer's *Canterbury Tales*. The group could then make a pilgrimage frieze. Each child could draw a person in the appropriate clothes of a particular period in history beginning with the first Roman pilgrims and ending with a picture of themselves. Others could draw the mode of transport of the time. At one end of the frieze draw a picture of St Alban's Abbey or St Alban. Then glue on in chronological order the different figures the children have made. If you have enough space, the children could produce life-size models by drawing around each other to create a pilgrim outline.

Roses for St Alban

According to Bede the place where Alban met his martyrdom was covered with flowers. One legend said that the drops of his blood became roses. The rose has become the symbol for St Alban and every year at St Alban's Abbey there is a special Rose Service to commemorate the saint on the Sunday following his festival on 22 June.

Children can make their own St Alban's roses from tissue paper or coloured paper tissues (see diagram).

1 Unfold two paper tissues and place them on top of one another.

2 Fold them in half as shown.

3 Cut along the fold.

4 Concertina the four strips as shown.

5 Fold in half and secure the centre with a staple.

6 Gently separate the pleats of tissue to form the petals.

7 You can then attach the completed rose to sticks or pipe-cleaners or pin them as they are to an altar frontal for St Alban's day. They can also be used as props in the drama.

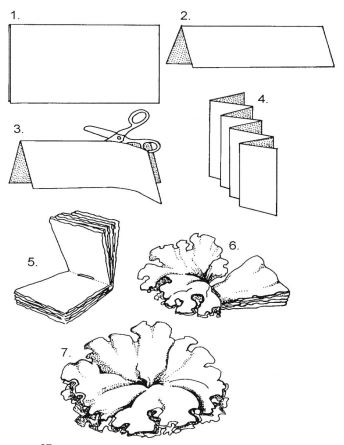

The Call to Repent

St JOHN THE BAPTIST

24 JUNE

Most saints are commemorated on the anniversary of their death; but St John the Baptist is celebrated on his birthday.

The figure of John is prominent in the early narratives of the gospels. His ministry prefigures that of Christ. John was a fearless man of uncompromising beliefs, a prophet with a clear mission to prepare the way for Christ. The birth of John, like that of Jesus, is foretold by an angel (Luke 1. 5-25) who instructed Zechariah that he should be called John. After the birth narrative (Luke 1.57-80) John's next appearance is on the banks of the River Jordan, warning people to repent and be baptised (Matt. 3.1-12, Mark 1.2-8, Luke 3.1-21). Jesus's baptism by John is recorded in the Synoptic Gospels, (Matt. 3.13-17, Luke 3. 21-22, Mark 1. 9-11). John's criticism of Herod Antipas for his marriage led to his imprisonment and subsequent beheading (Matthew 14.1-12, Mark 6.14-29, Luke 9.7-9). According to the Jewish historian Josephus, John was imprisoned and killed at the fortress of Machaerus by the Dead Sea.

Themes to explore with children

The life of John the Baptist is rich with the themes of light and darkness, sin and repentance, baptism and renewal. All these themes are present in the sacrament of baptism and this season is an appropriate time to look at this sacrament.

Before any themes are explored it is important that the children are made familiar with the life of John. Once the appropriate biblical passages have been read the children could be encouraged to act out John preaching by the River Jordan and baptising Jesus.

Not all children will be familiar with the service of baptism so it might be helpful to show them what happens and what is said.

To explore the following themes with them you will need copies of the templates shown, paper and drawing implements, baptism candles, matches, playdough or clay, a book on choosing a name for a new baby which gives the meaning of names.

LIGHT

In St John's Gospel the author refers to Jesus as the light of men (John 1.7-8). At a baptism service many churches present the godparents, or the newly baptised, with a lighted candle to symbolise that the new Christian is to 'shine as a light in the world to the glory of God the Father'. Show the group a lit baptism candle in its holder.

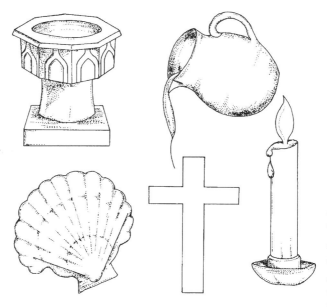

Templates for a baptism frieze

SIN AND REPENTANCE

John the Baptist demanded that people repent of their sins and be baptised. To help children understand a bit more about the concept of repentance, try this short exercise.

Discuss with the group what they consider to be a sin. Then ask each child to write down or draw a picture of the worst thing they have ever done. Ask them to fold up their papers. What are their feelings about the action now?

Then get each child to drop their piece of paper on a fireproof plate without disclosing what is on it. In front of all the group the teacher should set light to the pieces of paper. Explain that no-one else really knows

their sins except God alone and when people are sorry for what they have done God takes the sin away just as the fire burns up the paper.

WATER AND BAPTISM

Ask the children to consider the different uses of water: washing, cleaning, feeding plants and life, drinking, as a source of power, etc. They could then design a frieze which illustrates the different uses of water.

Once the general uses of water are established ask the children what the water of baptism is for. Read out the appropriate part in the baptism service. Explain that water at baptism is a Christian symbol for cleansing from sin, the beginning of a life with Christ and a new birth into the family of the church. When people are baptised they become members of the Church and are signed with a cross.

The water for baptism may be poured from a ewer or scallop shell. John the Baptist is often illustrated pouring water over Christ's head with a shell.

The shell is an ancient symbol of pilgrims. Go into your church and show the group the font, ewer or shell. If possible let them take part in a baptism service. Younger children might like to model a font out of clay or playdough. They can then draw a frieze to illustrate the baptism of Jesus and a baptism in their own church using the templates illustrated. Alternatively they might draw a design using the symbols of baptism and initiation into the Christian community.

CHRISTIAN NAMES

The story of the angel visiting Zechariah and telling him that his child should be called John, shows the importance attached to naming people in the ancient world. Although the giving of the name is independent of the act of baptism the name of a candidate may be used in the ceremony. Get the children to find out what their names mean and why they were given certain names. Each child can then each draw a picture of themselves fulfilling the meaning of their name.

Building On the Rock

S t Peter had many roles in life. He was brother, son-in-law, fisherman, disciple, 'rock', visionary, charismatic leader, healer and the heavenly gatekeeper. In church tradition he is also the patron of the Church and of the papacy. This great saint is remembered in the church calendar on 29 June. Most of what we know of him is found in the New Testament. He was called Simon Bar-Jonah and came from Bethsaida. He was called by Jesus with his brother Andrew to 'become fishers of men' (Mark 1. 17). After Peter's confession at Caesarea Philippi (Matt. 16. 13-20) Jesus says to him, 'You are Peter, and on this rock I will build my Church, and the powers of death shall not prevail against it. I will give you the keys of the kingdom of heaven.' (RSV). Although Peter was one of the inner band of disciples who witnessed the transfiguration and the agony in the Garden, he still denied knowledge of Jesus before Jesus's trial. After the resurrection Peter became the leader among the other apostles. Traditionally Petertide is the season for ordinations. This can broaden into a time when churches consider the priesthood of all believers. St Peter was a man who held many jobs or roles and these activity suggestions explore them.

Bible study

Read out Jesus's charge to Peter from Matthew 16. 13-19. Ask the group what they think Peter might have felt when Jesus gave him this office.

Explain that Jesus gave Peter a special responsibility. Ask the group if they have ever been given a special responsibility to do something or to look after someone? How did they feel? Were they worried, frightened or excited?

Who does what in the church?

Peter was one of the leaders of the early Church. Ask the children to think of the people who help in their church. What do they see as the main jobs in the church? Compile a simple questionnaire for them to fill in about who does what, where and when. Discuss the completed questionnaires with the group.

Younger children can take it in turns to mime the various jobs done by people in the church while the rest of the group guess what the job is. Older children can draw pictures or take photographs of the people who help in the church. They can mount the named pictures on a welcome board in the church porch.

Apprentice Sunday

Invite members of the congregation to come and talk about how they do their job in the church. If possible let the children have a go at pulling out the stops with the organist; shining with the polishers and taking a break with the coffee-makers.

Our church: a collage

Once you have explored the different jobs in the church discuss the idea of collective responsibility with the children. Ask them what would happen if, next Sunday, people with specific jobs did not turn up to church.

Explain that everyone has a job to do in church and the wider community. Not all functions are as clear as that of the vicar and the organist, but everyone has a part to play. Discuss with the group their individual participation in the family of the church. When they come and say their prayers and sing praise they are joining in the celebration of the whole church family.

To illustrate this, the group can make a collage. Take a large sheet of plain wallpaper. Draw an outline of your church. Then ask the group to draw pictures of the family of the church. These can be pictures of the people doing their work in the church, or in the community. Make sure the children remember to draw some people praying.

A net of talent

IDEAS FOR A FAMILY SERVICE

In Mark 1.17 Jesus said to Peter and Andrew 'I will make you become fishers of men.' Since the days of the early Church, fish have been a Christian symbol. Explore this image with the group before the service.

In advance of the service cut out enough paper fish-shapes to hand to each member of the congregation. Ask the children to prepare a short presentation about the jobs people do in church. During the presentation in the service the other children can hand out the fish-shapes and pencils to every member of the congregation. The leader should then ask the congregation to think of the job they do or the role they play in the church or community.

Ask the congregation to draw a symbol which represents this role on their fish-shape (use those illustrated as a guide), and to write their name on the fish. During the offertory the children can go around the congregation with fishing nets collecting the fish. These gifts of the whole family of the church can be offered up in prayer.

A Time for Asking Questions

The apostle Thomas is mentioned as one of the 12 disciples in all four gospels but it is in St John's Gospel that we find out more about him. Here he makes three appearances and is remembered as the one who dares to ask questions about Jesus's resurrection. For this reason he is often known as Doubting Thomas.

The feast day of Thomas the Apostle on 3 July is an appropriate time to look at the themes of questioning and doubt in faith with children. But first we must understand more about the apostle himself.

In St John's Gospel he is known as Didymus, the twin. When Jesus is on his way to Bethany, Thomas offers to die with him (John 11. 16). The second appearance is during the last discourse when Jesus assures the disciples that he is preparing a place for them so that they can be with him, Thomas asks: 'Lord, we do not know where you are going; how can we know the way?' (John 14. 5 RSV). Jesus replies to Thomas: 'I am the way, and the truth, and the life; no one comes to the Father, but by me.' His third appearance is when he doubts the resurrection of Christ (John 20. 25-28 RSV). Thomas is the first disciple to express explicitly the divinity of Christ in his response to Jesus: 'My Lord and my God' (John 20.28). On two occasions Thomas's questions lead to further revelation about the person of Jesus.

The India connection

Many traditions and a wealth of of apocryphal literature give clues about Thomas's later life. One tradition maintains that he was a missionary among the Parthians; another, that he was a missionary in India and met his martyrdom there. He is believed to have been killed with a spear and buried in Mylapore, near Madras. The Syrian Christians of Malabar believe that their ancestors were evangelised by Thomas when he landed in Cranganore in AD 52 and established seven churches. An ancient stone cross dating from between the sixth and eighth centuries known as the 'Thomas Cross' is preserved in a church where he was believed to have been buried and this has become the distinctive cross of this group of churches.

Activities for St Thomas's Day

Children are naturally questioning. Like St Thomas they want clear answers to difficult questions. The first two activities show how asking questions often helps us understand more about something, or reveals something more clearly to us.

Blindfold games

Thomas said he would accept the resurrection when he touched the wounds of Jesus. Ask the children to imagine what the disciples were thinking when they saw the risen Christ. What would they have wanted to say and do? Ask them to consider what they would have asked Jesus. What would make them sure of his resurrection?

Then get all the children in a circle. Take one child out of the group, blindfold him and guide him around the other children. The blindfolded child has to guess who everyone is just by touching. Once the blindfold is taken off the child clearly sees who he was touching. This can be repeated with each child in the group.

Objects rather than people can be used. All the children can be blindfolded and then a bag of objects can be passed around for the children to feel. Once they have all felt the bag then they can share what they believe the objects to be. When they take off their blindfolds the contents of the bag become clear. Each game enables the children to consider he importance of touch and then of sight to establish the reality of something.

Revealing jigsaws

Jigsaw games are a useful way to illustrate how a number of different things make up a complete picture or how questioning can reveal more about something. Before the class meets, find a clear photograph or picture of someone which can be mounted on card and cut up into a number of pieces. In the class place each separate piece reverse side down on the floor and ask the children to sit around it. Get the children to take it in turns to ask questions about who the person is. After every question is asked the child should turn over a piece of the jigsaw, whether they have guessed something correctly or not. Gradually the person is revealed through the questions and by the gradual revelation of the jigsaw.

A St Thomas Cross pendant

You will need copies of the template illustrated, scissors, card, thread or string.

The St Thomas Cross illustrated here is taken from a photograph of the cross on Saint Thomas Mount, Madras. Similar crosses are found in different areas of India. Each part of the cross is a symbol: the base is the throne of God; the rainbow, the covenant between God and humanity; the lotus shape, India; the cross is of Jesus and the dove above it of the Holy Spirit. The children can draw around the template on card adding a small eye to thread string through to make their own pendants.

In the Brotherhood of Christ

The Benedictine Rule, Benedictine monasteries and Benedictine men and women have had a profound and lasting effect on European Christianity, but we know few personal details about the 'Patriarch of Western Monasticism', St Benedict. His day falls on 11 July.

Benedict was born in 480 in Nursia (modern Norcia) in Italy. The main source for his life is the Dialogues of St Gregory (c 540-604). Benedict was educated in Rome but, repelled by the moral laxity he found there, he left before finishing his studies and went to live as a hermit in Subiaco. Here he met a monk called Romanus, who led him to a desolate cave. For three years Benedict lived a life of prayer there; Romanus brought him food and drink. Benedict attracted many followers: these he organised into 12 groups of 12 men and appointed an abbot for each community. He had to leave Subiaco in about 525 because of local jealousy, and he moved to Monte Cassino, near Naples.

On the summit of Monte Cassino he founded his famous monastery. Here he composed the final version of his Rule. This is influenced by the earlier Rules of Basil, John Cassian, the Desert Fathers, and the Rule of the Master. The Rule prescribes a life of prayer, study and work, lived socially in community. It combines spiritual teaching with practical directives for community life. Each day is organised around the seven-fold office. The community is overseen by an abbot who is chosen by the monks. The monastic vow demands stability of residence, obedience and monastic zeal. The Benedictine Rule was demanding but flexible and workable. The Rule spread from Italy through Western Europe to Britain and became the normative monastic code of Western Europe.

The writings of St Gregory tell of a holy abbot who helped all in the population, healing the sick, relieving those in distress and distributing alms and food to the poor. He is believed to have been buried in Monte Cassino in the same grave as his sister St Scholastica. But from the seventh century the Abbey at St Benoît-sur-Loire in France claimed to possess his relics.

Today there are hundreds of Benedictine Communities in the Roman Catholic and Anglican Churches. There are Anglican Benedictines, and communities which have adopted Benedictine vows or which are Benedictine in orientation throughout the Anglican Communion.

The features can be cut out of material, paper or wool. See diagram.

FOR OLDER CHILDREN

A day in the life of a modern Benedictine

Life in a modern Benedictine community retains the prayerful ordering of time, activity and reflection. The day is ordered around the sevenfold office. This is a typical weekday timetable of a monk at Alton Abbey:

5.30-6.00 am	vigil
6.00-6.30	meditation
6.30-7.10	lectio divina (reading)
7.15-7.40	morning prayer
7.45-8.00	breakfast
8.00-9.00	tidying up cell, reading newspapers
9.00-9.40	mass
9.40-10.10	coffee with community and guests
10.10-12.00	work (wafer-baking, incense making, computer typesetting, accounts, church work, domestic work)
12.00-12.15	midday office
12.15-12.45	lunch
12.45-1.30	rest
1.30-4.00	work
4.00-4.30	tea with community
4.30-5.00	tidy up work
5.00-5.40	evening prayer
5.40-6.00	TV news
6.00-6.30	supper
6.30-8.00	recreation/study
8.00-8.30	silent prayer
8.30-8.50	night prayer
9.00pm-5.30am	sleep

Make enlargements of the pictorial diary illustrated and give a copy to each child. Ask the children to draw the day of a monk at Alton Abbey on one of the diaries, showing what a monk does in each division of time. Then ask them to draw a pictorial diary for their own day. Discuss with them the time they have for prayer and worship. After they have taken time for sleep and school what else takes a big part of their day?

---

features cut out of material or paper — wool — hood — cut out card — string — card cut-out sandal — toilet roll covered with black material

FOR YOUNGER CHILDREN

A St Benedict model

In his Rule Benedict set out instructions for the simple attire of the monks. Younger children can learn something of the simplicity of the monastic lifestyle by making their own model of St Benedict.

Cover the inside of a toilet roll or kitchen roll with black cloth or paper to make the habit. The head can be made from table-tennis balls, or from a piece of stocking material stuffed with cotton wool and attached inside the tube.

Come Rain or Shine

*'St Swithin's day, if ye do rain, For forty days it will remain;
St Swithin's day, an ye be fair, for forty days 'twill rain nae mair.'*

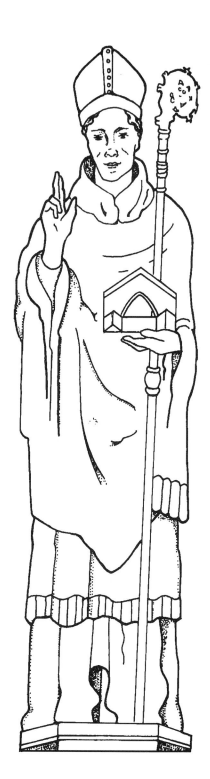

Of this ninth-century saint we know very little. He was Bishop of Winchester from 852 and adviser to Egbert, King of Wessex. He died in 862, leaving the request that he be buried in the churchyard of the minster so that the rain could fall upon his grave. All went well until he was canonized. Monks at Winchester then decided to remove his remains to a more prominent position in the priory church on 15 July 971. It rained all day and for the next 40 days.

Tradition maintains that this was the saint's way of showing his displeasure. Many miraculous cures at the time gave further proof of the saint's power. The saying runs that if it rains on St Swithin's day it will rain for the following 40 days.

There are a number of lives of the saint. From these we learn that Swithin was born in Wessex and educated at the Old Minster, Winchester. He was chosen by Egbert, King of Wessex from 802 to 839 as his chaplain. He also educated Ethelwulf, Egbert's son, who succeeded his father as king. Ethelwulf chose Swithin as Bishop of Winchester, a position he held for ten years until his death. Wessex was an important kingdom in the ninth century. Swithin became a well-known and popular bishop, celebrated for his charitable gifts and for his building of churches.

Winchester grew in importance as an ecclesiastical centre. A Benedictine monastery named after the saint was famous in the twelfth century for its writing of illuminated manuscripts. One of the most precious of these is The Winchester Bible.

Bookbinding

If you didn't make illuminated texts for St Bede's day you could do so for St Swithin's day instead. Alternatively a book of prayers which could incorporate illuminated texts is suggested here.

You will need two or three sheets of A4 paper, a sheet of A4 card, needle and cotton, Blu-Tak or plasticine, drawing materials including a gold or silver pen.

Fold the paper and card in half so that the card forms the cover. Stitch the sheets together with a needle and thread along the fold. Press the needle through the paper and card into a bit of plasticine or Blu-Tak so that the children don't prick their fingers. Ask the children to write out prayers they like, or prayers of their own composing on each page. In illuminated manuscripts the main illustrations were usually around the initial letter. The decorations can be made in felt-tip pen or with paint and a gold pen.

Statues

The line drawing is of a statue of St Swithin from the Great Screen behind the High Altar in Winchester Cathedral. The statue of St Swithin is one of many on the screen. He carries a bridge because it is believed that he had many bridges built to help travellers. The group can model their own statues out of clay, playdough or plasticine. They could choose their favourite saint. Ask them to think of the symbols which might be associated with that person and incorporate them into the model. When they have finished their models you could create your own screen.

A weather chart

Divide a large sheet of paper or card into 40 boxes, and number them. Divide your group up so that each child is given a number of days on which to be responsible for recording the weather.

Make a note of the weather on St Swithin's day, and ask the group to draw a picture of St Swithin with the weather on his day.

At the beginning of each session after St Swithin's day the children can record the weather of the past week on the chart. Alternatively the children can take it in turns to take the chart home to keep a record.

At the end of the 40 days, is there any pattern on their chart?

With an older age group you could make a rain-gauge and check the rainfall level each day.

A Friend of Jesus

St MARY MAGDALENE

22 JULY

Mary Magdalene was a devoted follower of Jesus. She first appears in St Luke's Gospel (8.2) where we learn that 'seven demons had gone out' from her. We are also told that she and other women 'provided for him out of their means'. Her next appearance is not until the crucifixion and resurrection narratives. She is one of those at the foot of the cross (Mark 15.40) and with others she discovers the empty tomb and hears of the resurrection (Mark 16.1). She is also the first to see the risen Christ (John 20 1ff: Mark 16.9).

In Christian tradition Mary Magdalene has also been identified as the sinner who anointed Jesus at Simon's house (Luke 7.37) and with Mary the sister of Martha who also anointed him (John 12.3).

Scriptural evidence is lacking, but Mary Magdalene is often depicted as a sensuous woman who carries a jar of ointment.

After the resurrection, according to Eastern Church tradition, Mary went with the Blessed Virgin Mary and St John to Ephesus, where in time she died. In Western legend, by contrast, she came to the south of France with Martha and Lazarus and evangelised Provence, living as a hermit in the Maritime Alps before she died at Saint Maximin.

a Fill the foot of a stocking or sock with stuffing to make a face, and secure with string.

b Cut out a 50 cm x 20cm piece of material or felt and fold in half.

c Cut along the dotted lines and sew edges together. Pierce a small hole in the top of the figure as shown.

d Insert the head and sew into the body.

e Add details of face, hair, clothes.

Teaching about friendship

Because she was one of Jesus's friends, Mary Magdalene's feast day on 22 July provides an opportunity to explore with children the theme of friendship. Talk about how friendship grows. Ask the children how they make friends. Why do we need friends and what do we gain from them?

Discuss Jesus's friends, and point out that some were women, Mary Magdalene being one of them. The following activities explore the theme of friendship and help children remember some of the incidents in St Mary's life.

A friendship chain

You will need strips of coloured paper, felt-tip pens, glue or sticky tape.

Discuss with the group how our friendship with others and with Jesus binds us together. This can be illustrated by getting the children to make a friendship chain.

Using some bought or cut-out paper-chain strips, ask the children to write their own names on the middle of a strip. Then get them to write the names of two of their friends on two more strips. Make a chain out of these three strips with the names facing outwards. Using a different coloured strip get each child to write JESUS on a strip. These JESUS strips can then be used to join the friendship chains to make a continuous chain. Display this in church with the banner, 'We Thank God For Our Friends'.

A drama or puppet theatre

You will need dressing-up clothes, copies of the templates illustrated, drawing materials, card, sticky tape, lolly sticks, stockings or socks, stuffing, string, materials, needle and thread, and glue.

First recount the main incidents in Mary Magdalene's life, or get the older children to read them themselves.

1 Her healing and following of Jesus (Luke 8.2, Mark 16.9).

2 At the crucifixion and burial of Jesus (Matt. 27.55, Mark 15.40-47, John 19.25).

3 Preparing spices to take to the tomb when the Sabbath was over (Luke 23. 56).

4 Visiting the tomb and meeting the risen Christ (Luke 24.10, John 20.1, 11-18, Mark 16.1-11, Matt. 28.1-10).

Provide simple dressing-up clothes and let the children divide into small groups to act out each incident.

Alternatively two simple puppets of Jesus and Mary Magdalene could be made and then the incidents acted out with these. For simple stick puppets for younger children use copies of the template. Then get each child to colour in the figures, and secure on lolly sticks with sticky tape.

Older children can make hand puppets. (The figures refer to the illustration). You will need careful adult supervision for this activity.

FOR YOUNGER CHILDREN

Mary Magdalene's album

You will need an inexpensive A4 photograph album or scrapbook, and drawing materials.

Encourage the children to illustrate the incidents from Mary's life and put their finished 'photographs' with captions in an album or scrapbook. These finished books could be displayed in church on 22 July until the following week.

43

The Great European Pilgrimage

James is one of the church's great heroes. He is the patron saint of Spain, Guatemala, and Nicaragua. Over the centuries millions have made pilgrimages to see his relics at Compostela in Spain.

About this great apostle we know very little. He was the son of Zebedee and brother of John. James and John were part of the inner circle of disciples who were present at the Transfiguration and in Gethsemane. Like his father and brother, James was a fisherman and worked with Simon and Andrew (Luke 5.10). He accepted the call to discipleship from Jesus (Matt. 4.21 and Mark 1.19). The nickname 'Sons of Thunder' (Mark 3.17) gives a clue as to the temperament of the two brothers. According to the New Testament, St James was the first of the Twelve to suffer martyrdom. He was beheaded by Herod Agrippa I (Acts 12.2).

From the seventh century there was a tradition that St James preached the gospel in Spain. Although this contradicts the New Testament which indicates that the apostles did not leave Jerusalem until after James's death the tradition survived. According to another legend the body of St James was translated to Santiago (which means 'St James') de Compostela in North West Spain. In the Middle Ages St James was one of the most popular Spanish saints and Compostela became the principal pilgrimage centre in Europe. In 1170 the military Order of Santiago, under the patronage of St James, was founded to fight the Moors.

The emblem of St James is the scallop shell. In the Middle Ages pilgrims wore these shells on their hats as a sign of their pilgrimage to Compostela. Today the scallop shell can be seen in the logos of Churches Together in England and The Council of Churches for Britain and Ireland.

The festival of St James falls within the holiday season and these activities are designed with this in mind. The suggestions focus on the themes of pilgrimage, the seashore, and summer games.

Pilgrimage ideas

Discuss with the children the idea of a pilgrimage as a special religious journey – one that refreshes and renews the Christian in his or her life journey through life. Ask them to think of pilgrimages they might have heard about e.g. in *The Canterbury Tales*, in *Pilgrim's Progress*, the quest for the Holy Grail, a trip to Taizé.

During the holiday season you could arrange a pilgrimage journey around the churchyard or the parish. The group could map out places of special religious significance. The children could hunt for different types of crosses and draw them. They might like to collect the names of saints on street names, shops, churches, and house names. Younger children can be given a card bearing their own name and then hunt down names which begin with the letters in their name.

Sea and shells

Take a scallop shell into the class. Ask the children to explore the church and church-yard to see if they can find any shells. Some churches might use the shell at a baptism

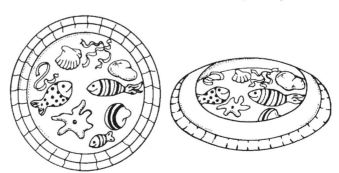

service. Others might have the symbol on masonry or carvings. The children can make their own scallop shells by moulding play-dough, flour dough or clay inside a scallop

shell. The model can be dried and decorated as a reminder of their own Christian journey.

Another idea is for the whole group to make a collage using cut-out shell shapes around a picture of St James.

The children can also make their own Sea of Galilee picture. If you live near a beach collect small shells, bits of seaweed, pebbles and sand. Alternatively you can use pasta shells, pebbles and cut-out paper shapes of seaweed.

You will need to provide each child with two paper plates, clear plastic and PVA glue. They should cut the centre out of one of plates. With the rim of the plate right side up, glue the plastic across the opening to create a window. Then colour the bottom of the uncut plate blue. On this 'sea' they can glue pebbles, sand, small shells (or pasta shapes), seaweed and paper fish to create a sea effect on the uncut plate. Cover this with the upside-down cut plate and staple the two plates together. See the diagram.

Sports for St James's Day

As it is the holiday season here are two games with a St James theme.

A ST JAMES ROWING RACE

Sit two teams down facing the starting line, and their backs towards the finish. Each 'rower' should have their legs apart with the person in front sitting between them. When the whistle is blown the person at the front of the team should run round to the back and sit down. This is repeated so that the team gradually moves towards the finishing line.

THE GOOD NEWS RELAY

Choose a biblical text and write it down for each team. Arrange the teams so that they do a relay race. Instead of passing a baton they have to whisper the biblical text. Give a prize to the team which passes on the Good News most accurately.

The King who fought for Christ

St Oswald was an archetypal Christian king. He fought for good, and God was seen to be on his side. He is remembered in the Church on 5 August.

Oswald was the son of Ethelfrith, King of Northumbria. When Ethelfrith died in 616, Edwin seized the kingdom and Oswald fled to Scotland, where he was educated by the monks on Iona.

Oswald's conversion and education on Iona had a profound impact on Northumbria. After Edwin died in 633 Oswald returned to his kingdom. He led his people into battle against the British king whom Bede called a 'savage tyrant', Cadwalla, at Heavenfield, near Hexham.

Before Oswald went into battle he erected a wooden cross on the battlefield and demanded that his soldiers pray. 'Let us kneel together, and ask the true and living God Almighty of His mercy to protect us from the arrogant savagery of our enemies, since He knows that we fight in a just cause to save our nation' (Bede). Oswald and his troops won the battle. Oswald also won converts for Christianity. He sent a request to Iona for a missionary to help him establish Christianity in his kingdom. The first bishop found the Northumbrians barbaric and obstinate, and he did not stay long. He was replaced by Aidan.

Oswald accompanied Aidan on many of his preaching trips and acted as his translator. He gave Aidan Lindisfarne as his see; and this island became a centre for Christian teaching and learning. He also gave money and lands to establish other monasteries where his English subjects were instructed in the Christian faith.

King Oswald also made important political advances in the region. He united both parts of Northumbria, Bernicia and Deira. But Oswald's reign did not last long. He was killed in battle by King Penda of Mercia at the Battle of Maserfield when he was only 38. Penda ordered that his body be multilated and hung up on stakes.

A generous king Bede records that King Oswald was 'always wonderfully humble, kindly, and generous to the poor and strangers.' He tells the story of how on one Easter feast Oswald was sitting down to dine with Bishop Aidan when a servant came in and informed the king about how a great crowd of poor people were sitting outside begging alms from him. Oswald ordered his own food to be taken out to the poor, his silver dish broken up and distributed to them.

Story Plates

Ask the children to act out the story of King Oswald's silver plate. Remind them that King Oswald was a rich man who recognised that all he had came from God and was to be shared. Discuss with the group how they can share their riches today. This might be by giving to charity or by giving of their time. After the discussion give each child a paper plate. On one side ask them to draw a picture of King Oswald giving his food and plate to the poor. On the other side of the plate they can make a collage or draw a picture of how they can share what they have received.

A warrior for Christ

King Oswald fought against the pagan kings Cadwalla and Penda. He was brave and courageous in battle. You can ask the children to design King Oswald's shield. What is a suitable emblem for him? Which incidents from his life could be illustrated on the shields?

The Lindisfarne legacy

St Oswald gave St Aidan Lindisfarne island to set up his monastery. Forty-seven years after Aidan's death a monk at Lindisfarne set himself the task of writing the four Gospels in Latin and these became known as the *Lindisfarne Gospels*. These books are fine examples of the Celtic art of the time. The manuscripts were written to glorify God. Using the illustrations given ask the children to design the front cover of a story book about King Oswald in the Celtic style.

The Feast of The Transfiguration

The Feast of the Transfiguration on 6 August focuses on the themes of the revelation of the divinity of Christ, his fulfilment of the Old Testament and his future destiny and heavenly glory. These ideas present the teacher with a challenge that calls for careful preparation.

The story of the Transfiguration is recorded in each of the Synoptic Gospels (Matt. 17.1-9, Mark 9.2-10, Luke 9.28-36). Although there are small differences in each account they all agree on the four main points: Jesus was transfigured or that his appearance and face changed; that Moses and Elijah appeared with him; God declared Jesus as his son and that the event was witnessed by Peter, James and John. Traditionally the Transfiguration was believed to have taken place on Mount Tabor but many scholars today prefer Mount Hermon as the site.

Read the children the Lucan account of the story. Then explore the following themes with them.

Light

At the Transfiguration the light on Christ is dazzling and transforms his face and clothes. Explore the symbolism of light with children.

FOR OLDER CHILDREN

Darken a room and ask everyone to sit very still as you light a candle. Encourage the children to pick out the colours of the light so that they settle down.

1   Then ask them what the light does to the room. Get them to write up their answers on a large sheet of paper. Their answers may include words like lightens, brightens, warms, cheers.

2   Then ask them what the light does to people's faces. Again they can write their responses on the paper. These may include words like watching, concentrating, gazing.

Explain that light can be a symbol of God's love radiating through Christ. Like the light in the room Christ's love can transform people. The disciples, like the children, were transfixed by the light. Once you have established the link between light and Christ, ask the children to think of people who radiate love. Can any of them think of times when people's lives are transformed by love?

FOR YOUNGER CHILDREN

Provide the children with greaseproof paper and felt-tipped pens. Ask them to draw Moses, Elijah and Christ from the story. Then hold the finished pictures carefully in front of a candle flame. Ask them what the light does to the pictures. Does it change or brighten them? Then explain that the light is like God's love as it brightens and changes the people in the picture.

High and holy places

Ask the children why Moses and Elijah appeared with Jesus on the mountain. Read to them or remind them of the story of Moses receiving the Ten Commandments (Exodus 24.9-18 and 34. 29-35). Get them to write down the similarities between the Transfiguration and the Moses story. In both, God appears on a mountain and his presence is expressed as light. Explain that Moses represents the Law and Elijah the Prophets. Christ is the fulfilment of both the Law and the Prophets. Moses and Elijah also suggest Christ's own exodus and future glory.

The ancients believed that high places were closer to God, and therefore when God appeared it was often on a hill or mountain. Ask the older children to think about other occasions in the New Testament when Jesus is with God in a high place. They may remember the Mount of Olives, the Crucifixion and the Ascension.

The Transfiguration shows, before Jesus suffers and dies, that he is God. The same three disciples are with Jesus at the Transfiguration and at the Mount of Olives before Jesus is betrayed. Read the children the ASB collect for the day:

'Almighty Father, whose Son was revealed in majesty before he suffered death upon the cross: give us faith to perceive his glory, that we may be strengthened to suffer with him and be changed into his likeness, from glory to glory; who is alive and reigns with you and the Holy Spirit, one God, now and for ever.'

Discuss with them why it was important for the disciples to be given this sign that Jesus was God before he was crucified.

A Transfiguration mobile

A mobile of the transfiguration links the themes of light and high places.

You will need copies of the templates illustrated, straws, foil, glue, colouring materials, string, scissors.

Get the children to copy the templates of the figures. They can colour in the figures and glue foil to the figure of Christ so that it catches the light. Attach each of the figures to string, as shown, and hang from a drinking straw covered with the cloud shape. The mobile should be hung near a window so that it catches the light.

Transfiguration mobile

The Price of Walking with God

St Bartholomew is one of those popular apostles about whom little is known for certain, but who has inspired a wealth of legend and tradition. Bartholomew is mentioned in all the Synoptic Gospels (Mark 3.18, Luke 6.14, Matt.10.3) and in the book of Acts (1.13), but we are given few clues about his personality or background. The name Bartholomew is a patronymic meaning 'son of Tolmai', and so he may have had another name; and since the the ninth century he has been identified with Nathanael (John 1.45-51, 21.2), the disciple from Cana whom Jesus commended for his sincerity.

According to the church historian Eusebius, when Pantaenus of Alexandria visited India between AD 150 and 200 he found a 'Gospel according to Matthew' in Hebrew which had been left behind by 'Bartholomew, one of the Apostles'. Other traditions link him with Armenia. He is said to have been flayed alive before being beheaded at Derbend on the Caspian Sea. Tradition maintains that, after being flayed, he was hung on a cross to die and exposed to the flies.

The popularity of his cult in England is largely due to Queen Emma, King Canute's wife, who presented the apostle's arm to Canterbury. He also appears in the *Life of Guthlac* by Felix. St Bartholomew's Hospital in London was founded in 1123 by a monk named Rahere who had been miraculously cured in Rome by a visitation of the apostle. When he returned from his pilgrimage he set up a hospice for the sick.

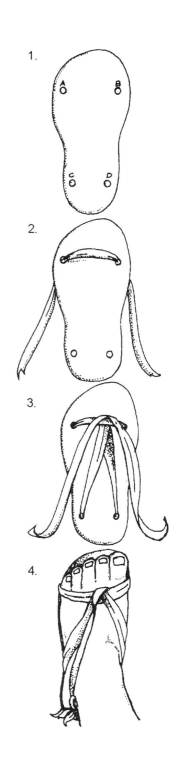

By association with his own fate, Bartholomew is patron saint of butchers, tanners, shoemakers and bee-keepers. He is often pictured holding a flaying-knife. While some children might have a fascination for the more grisly aspects of Bartholomew's death they provide the teacher with little immediate teaching material. Perhaps concentrate instead on his patronage.

Apostles are followers of Jesus, people sent out by him who walk in his footsteps.

Sandal-making

You will need cardboard, scissors, drawing materials and ribbons or tape.

Get the children to draw around their own feet on a piece of stiff card. Leave 1cm border around the foot shape and cut out two soles. Make the holes shown in the diagram within the border area. Each child should then place their feet in the soles and thread the ribbon through the sandals as shown in the diagram.

You now have a rough-and-ready apostle ready to follow in the steps of Christ and go out on a missionary adventure.

Christian path poster

This activity aims to get people to think of the different stages in their own life and what following in the steps of Christ might entail. It can be adapted for different age groups. The footsteps on the Christian path can refer to an individual as here, a family or the life of a church community. The material is appropriate for use on the festivals of other apostles.

You will need a large sheet of paper or wall-paper and drawing materials.

Get the group to draw a series of footsteps on the wallpaper by drawing around their own feet. Then discuss with them the different stages of their life: their birth, starting school, work, etc. On each foot shape get them to draw a picture or symbol of that stage in their lives. Then they should draw in a foot shape their present stage. Get them to draw a dotted line across their footstep path and then consider the different stages of their life in future. Again they can draw a picture or symbol in each foot shape.

Once the footstep poster is completed you can discuss how St Bartholomew might have filled in his poster. Discuss with the group what following the Christian way means in their lives. What are the stages in the Christian life? Does their poster reflect the journey of a follower of Christ?

The group might like to incorporate songs into their activity. Suitable ones would be: *One more step along the world I go; O for a closer walk with God; Two little eyes to look to God; O Jesus, I have promised.*

The Gentle Missionary who spoke his Mind

The stories of Aidan and the other Northumbrian saints recorded in Bede's *A History of the English Church and People* have retained their rich vividness through the centuries. These are the holy adventurers. Their message is clear, their evangelism uncompromising.

Aidan's influence was widespread but he has often been forgotten in later church history. The monasteries and schools Aidan set up helped nurture the church in Northumbria at a time when it was the greatest of the Anglo-Saxon kingdoms. Most of the North and Midlands was evangelised by monks and nuns who owed their allegiance to Lindisfarne.

St Aidan lived in the seventh century. Like King Oswald of Northumbria, he was educated at Iona in Scotland. Oswald wanted his subjects to share his Christian faith and called upon Iona to supply him with a missionary. The first man they sent had little success amongst the people and he returned to Iona. Aidan was then chosen to help King Oswald.

According to Bede, Aidan was a man of outstanding gentleness, holiness and moderation. Oswald gave him Lindisfarne as his see (now called Holy Island), a small island off the Northumbrian coast near today's Berwick. Aidan worked with Oswald to preach the gospel. As Aidan was 'not fluent in the English language', Oswald acted as translator on these missionary journeys. Bede records that Aidan was an 'inspiring example of self-discipline and continence' to his clergy. 'He never sought or cared for any worldly possession, and loved to give away to the poor whatever he received from kings or wealthy folk.' Aidan travelled everywhere on foot speaking to everyone he met on the way. If they were pagan he urged them to be baptised. All who went with him were required to meditate and read the Scriptures.

He was also a man of uncompromising beliefs. If asked to dine with the king, he would eat sparingly and always leave as soon as possible to pray. We are told he sometimes went to pray in solitude on the island of Inner Farne. Money given to him by the rich he handed on to the poor, or used it to ransom slaves. Bede tells the story that King Oswin gave Bishop Aidan a fine horse for his work. When a poor man asked Aidan for alms the bishop dismounted and gave the beggar the horse. When King Oswin (Oswald's successor) questioned Aidan about giving away such a valuable horse to a beggar, the bishop replied: 'What are you saying, your majesty? Is this foal of a mare more valuable to you than the Son of God?'

Aidan died on 31 August 651 and was buried on Lindisfarne.

A Lindisfarne monastery

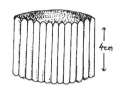

Aidan's Monastery

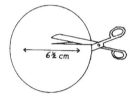

You will need the inside of a kitchen or toilet roll, matchsticks, circles of card, glue and perhaps pipe-cleaners.

The monastery at Lindisfarne was probably a series of round, wooden thatched buildings (see drawing). The monks would have come together for worship in a simple church. Models of the monastery can be made to help children appreciate the simplicity of monastic life. Cut the kitchen/toilet roll into 4cm lengths. Cut the ends off the matchsticks and get the children to stick these around the roll. Older children might like to make a doorway, sticking the matchsticks on afterwards. Then cut a circle of card 6.5cm in diameter and cut out a small segment as shown. This should be glued to form a pointed roof and be rested on the cardboard roll to form a monastery. You could add tiny scraps of material or wood to the roof to make it more effective.

A church can be modelled out of a fruit juice box, using a similar method, and pipe-cleaner figures can be placed inside the huts.

The gospel in Northumbria board game

You will need felt-tipped pens and drawing materials, sheets of A4 paper or card divided into squares, a large sheet of card, dice and counters.

Tell the children the story of St Aidan. Ask them to devise a board game using the sheets of squared paper which you have provided. They need to illustrate the ups and downs of Aidan's life and work; for example:

● You have to learn a new language to speak to the local people: miss two goes.

● Two new people join the monastery: move on three places.

The action squares should then be stuck on a large piece of card and interspersed with blank squares to form a board game. The completed game can be played by all the children.

FOR YOUNGER CHILDREN
Aidan's horse

Tell the story about Aidan giving away the horse that Oswin had given him. Ask them how they would feel if someone had given away a gift which they had carefully chosen. Can they understand why Aidan gave away the horse? Tell the story again and encourage the children to pull appropriate faces for the different characters in the story as it is told. The story could also be acted out.

The Mother of Jesus

THE BLESSED VIRGIN MARY

8 SEPTEMBER

Mary, the mother of Jesus, is remembered on a number of occasions in the church calendar: the fourth Sunday in Advent; Christmas; the Annunciation on 25 March; and her birthday on 8 September. Most children are familiar with Mary through their school nativity play. The challenge for the children's worker is to get behind the plaster-cast crib model and the two-dimensional nativity play character to help children think about who Mary was and her importance in Jesus's life.

Explore the New Testament Gospel narratives for mentions of Mary. You can use these references as a guide: the annunciation (Luke 1.26-38); Mary telling Elizabeth of the birth (Luke 1.39-56); the birth narrative and the visit to Jerusalem (Luke 2); Jesus's family (Matt. 13.55-56); the wedding feast at Cana (John 2.1-11) and the Crucifixion (John 19.25-27).

FOR YOUNGER CHILDREN

A hyacinth as a prayer

Seeds and bulbs are particular gifts which God gives us to plant and to care for. Planting a hyacinth bulb can remind children of the Blessed Virgin Mary in special ways.

- The bulb can remind them of God's gifts to Mary of his son, Jesus.
- Their care as it grows can remind them of Mary's love and care for the growing Jesus.
- The hyacinth flower can remind them how Mary's love for Jesus flowered in his special love for all.
- Its scent can remind the children of God's love spreading among us because of the care and love Mary gave Jesus from the time he was a tiny baby until he suffered on the cross.

You will need a hyacinth bulb, gravel, compost, a saucer, a pot and a pot cap.

1. Put a layer of gravel in the bottom of the pot.
2. Half fill the pot with compost.
3. Put the bulb, pointed end up, on the compost.
4. Now fill the pot with moist compost to just below the bulb end.
5. Now water the pot, placing it on a saucer.
6. Make a hat for the pot. Take a thick piece of cardboard and draw a circle about twice the size of the pot top. Cut a slit to the centre. Then overlap the cut edges and staple or glue them. The hat can be decorated.

7. Put the pot in a cool spot until the bulb sprouts. Then uncover and water whenever the compost seems dry.

The children may like to take the sprouting hyacinth pot to church and put it in the area where the Christmas crib usually goes.

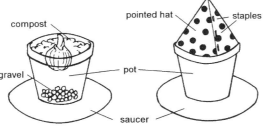

FOR OLDER CHILDREN

A prayer candle

We think of the love shared in families when we think of the Blessed Virgin Mary; a family candle can help children appreciate this. The candle can be painted in different bands, one for each member of the family. As it burns down, each becomes the focus of thought or prayer. Make sure there is always an adult to supervise the children with lit candles.

You will need a large, preferably stubby, white candle, a secure holder, string, non-flammable paint which can be applied to non-porous surfaces, a paintbrush.

1. Mark the candle in equal widths.

2. Leave the candle's top clear for at least one width.
3. Tie pieces of string to separate each width.
4. Paint each width a different colour or design. Let the paint dry and remove the pieces of string.

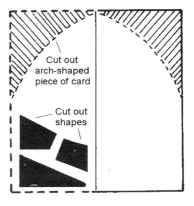

A stained-glass window

A stained-glass window depicting important moments in the Blessed Virgin Mary's life with Jesus can be a beautiful celebration of Mary's faithful love for her son.

Using the references given find out what the Gospels tell us about Mary. As the children read out the passages get them to think of a simple way to represent each event. Keep the pictures as simple as possible.

You will need a large piece of dark-coloured lightweight card, scissors, greaseproof paper, glue and coloured felt-tip markers.

1. Fold the card lengthways and cut out a curve from the open side of the top corner of the folded edge.
2. Glue one side of the card arch.
3. Spread the greaseproof paper and carefully press the glued surface of the card on to it.
4. Draw your design on the greaseproof paper.
5. Use the markers to colour the greaseproof paper, using smooth, even strokes. Strong colours will look paler when the light shines through. Coloured cellophane can also be used. Trim each piece to fit each separate pane. Using a black felt-pen fill in any gaps.
6. The finished work can be put on a window so that the light shines through.

Our Daily Bread

This Allsorts explores the theme and image of bread as a symbol of all we have to be grateful for at harvest. The material does not look at the bread of the Eucharist because to do so would demand a number of Allsorts; but leaders might want to adapt this material to include references to the Eucharist.

The richness of creation

At harvest we give thanks for the richness and variety of creation. We thank God for providing 'our daily bread'. Today our daily bread is usually more than just bread, and encompasses all foods. But bread remains the staple food in many societies and cultures. By looking and tasting different types of bread from around the world the children can begin to appreciate something of the richness of God's creation.

A week before the session, ask the children to bring in some bread next time. It can be a roll, a slice, a loaf, etc. The leader can collect unusual sorts of bread such as pitta, ciabatta, rye, chapati, soda, all of which are readily available in large supermarkets.

The following Sunday discuss the different types of bread with the group.

● Where does this sort of bread originally come from?

● Has it yeast in it?

● What sort of flour is it made from?

● Are there any other ingredients in it?

Divide the samples between the group and compare texture, taste and smell.

If facilities and time allow you could make different types of bread with the group. A simple recipe is given below. This could then form part of a harvest breakfast or supper or be used in a harvest service.

Alternatively, make an enlargement of the template of the map of the world. Ask the group to label the continents and draw in the sea. Then ask them to make pictures of all the different breads they have tasted and seen. They can then mount these pictures on the map on their countries of origin.

Leaven in the lump

Read Luke 13.20. Jesus said the kingdom of God was like yeast in a lump of dough. Discuss with the group how many of them have made bread or know how yeast works.

Let the group look at the effect of yeast by making their own bread. This recipe is for simple wholemeal bread. The cooking will need careful adult supervision. The dough only needs 30 minutes to rise and requires no kneading.

INGREDIENTS

3lb of stone-ground wholemeal flour
2 teaspoons of salt
2 packets of easy blend dried yeast
3 teaspoons of honey or brown sugar
2 pints of hand-hot water.

METHOD

1 Mix the flour and salt.

2 Stir in the yeast and honey or sugar.

3 Slowly stir in the water and mix thoroughly until the dough leaves the sides of the bowl and feels elastic.

4 Divide among three greased and floured loaf-tins.

5 Explain to the children that if there was no yeast in the flour the loaves would stay the same size and shape as they are now. Cover the loaves and put them in a warm place for about 30 minutes so that the dough rises within half an inch of the tin rim. Show the group the loaves. A small amount of yeast has spread to all parts of the flour and had a powerful effect on it. Jesus used the metaphor of yeast to show how God's reign often works in unseen ways but like yeast it spreads and has a powerful effect.

6 Then bake the loaves at Gas 6 or 400°/F for about 40 minutes.

Bread for the world

Harvest is often a time when the Churches focus on the needs of all God's people, especially on the people in the Third World. Agencies like Christian Aid provide materials which show how dependent the Western world is on Third World produce, and how unfair trading agreements can benefit richer countries.

For this activity the leader will need to have some knowledge of where certain foods are produced.

To illustrate the dependency of the West on the Third World set out a harvest breakfast for your group. Take in the bread you have made, coffee, tea, cocoa, bananas, sugar-coated cereals, etc.

The children can choose their own breakfast. Then ask them to say a grace giving thanks for this breakfast and for the people who helped make it. After they have eaten it, ask them to think about where their breakfast came from. What percentage was made entirely in this country? What percentage came from abroad?

Give each child a sheet of paper. Ask them to draw a picture of their breakfast and to write on each item of food where it came from. What would be left of their breakfast if all food made outside Britain was taken away?

Older children could take this exercise further. Encourage them to find out more about where their food comes from, the conditions of the producers and who determines the price of the raw ingredients. You could introduce Traidcraft or Tearcraft goods to the group.

Ways of Recalling the Cross

Holy Cross Day, also known as the Exaltation of the Cross, is a feast in honour of the cross of Christ. Its history is chequered. In the Western Church the day commemorates the exposition of the cross at Jerusalem in AD 629 by the Emperor Heraclius, when he recovered it from the Persians. But historians believe that this event actually took place in the spring. The 14 September date more likely belongs to an earlier commemoration – of the dedication of the basilica of the Holy Sepulchre, built by the Emperor Constantine, in AD 335. St Cyril of Jerusalem says that the Cross was found at Jerusalem during the time of Constantine; some suggest that this happened during the excavations for the basilica, and that the relic was housed in the new church. In the Greek Church the Feast of the Finding of the Cross was originally kept on 14 September together with the consecration of Constantine's two basilicas in Jerusalem.

In legend, the Cross of Christ is said to have been discovered by St Helena, Constantine's mother, on her pilgrimage to the Holy Land. Parts of the 'cross' were distributed to churches around the world. The medieval belief that St Helena was a native of England is now thought unlikely to be true, but St Helena has inspired British writers from the Anglo-Saxon poet Cynewulf to Evelyn Waugh in his historical novel, *Helena*.

Whatever the truth behind the legend, and whenever the relic of the cross was found, the cross has been a symbol of Christ, his crucifixion and humankind's redemption for centuries. For children Holy Cross Day can provide an opportunity for looking more carefully at the symbol, and the different shapes of crosses. They can also understand something of the importance of crafting their own crosses.

reminder that Christ is involved in every aspect of their lives.

FOR OLDER CHILDREN

A Celtic wool cross

Show the Celtic cross illustrated to the group. What do they notice about the lines? For the Celts, the presence of Christ is woven into people's lives like the Celtic patterns on stones, illuminated manuscripts and crosses.

The group can make a similar Celtic pattern by weaving a wool cross. Get three different colours of wool. Cut three 31cm lengths of each of the three colours. Then cut three 26cm lengths of each of the three colours.

Tie the nine strands of 31cm lengths together, plait the three colours, and secure. Then similarly plait together the smaller lengths. Strap the two lengths together to form a cross. This can then be hung on a wall, or made into a card.

During the summer holidays ask the children to collect or draw as many different-shaped crosses as they can find. Cross shapes can be identified with the help of the book *Saints, Signs and Symbols* by W. Ellwood Post (SPCK 0 281 02894 X).

For Holy Cross Day the children can make their own crosses, using the examples they have found or those in the illustration.

FOR OLDER CHILDREN

Model crosses

To make salt dough mix together 4 cups of flour, 1 cup of salt, 2 tbs oil, and about 1.5 cups of water, to make a dough. Give each child enough dough to model their own cross shapes. To decorate the crosses before baking the children can mark shapes into the dough.

Once the salt dough models are completed the teacher can bake them 4-8 hours in a cool oven. If not already decorated they can then be cooled and painted. By including a hole in the original cross shape these dough crosses can be hung or made into a mobile.

FOR YOUNGER CHILDREN

Mosaic crosses

Make a simple outline of a large Latin cross for each child. Divide the cross shape into a large mosaic using black felt-tip pen, leaving the centre bare. The children can then draw Christ in the middle of their cross. In the other segments they can draw simple pictures of things they do at home and at school. The finished mosaic cross can then serve as a

CELTIC

LATIN

MALTESE

CANTERBURY

GREEK

RUSSIAN ORTHODOX

Making the Feathers Fly

Hildegard of Bingen was an extraordinary naturalist, playwright, poetess and composer, as well as mystic. She lived in the twelfth century. She is remembered in many churches on 17 September.

Hildegard was born in 1098 to a noble family in Bockelheim on the River Nahe. When she was eight her parents put her into the care of a religious friend of the family, Jutta von Spanheim. Hildegard followed Jutta's instruction and at the age of 15 took religious vows. After Jutta's death Hildegard became abbess of the convent, which later moved to Rupertsberg near Bingen on the Rhine.

Since her childhood Hildegard had received visions from God. At the age of 42 she was told by God to write down all that she had seen and heard. *Scivias* which means 'Know the ways' or 'May you know', was the result. This book recounts the visions she received in words and pictures. While she was writing it, the Trier Synod of 1147 read out part of her work, and both Bernard of Clairvaux and Pope Eugenius III encour-

From a miniature drawn by Hildegard to accompany the forward of the Scivias. The flames of the Holy Ghost descend upon her. She writes her visions down on a wax tablet, which balances on her knee. The monk is Volmar who was her teacher.

aged her to continue. *Scivias* was written over ten years. The end of the book depicts a battle between good and evil which Hildegard set to music – *Ordo Virtutum, the play of the Virtues* – which is believed to be the earliest liturgical morality play.

Hildegard's fame spread. She was a prolific writer and her correspondents include emperors, bishops, kings, monks and nuns and people at all levels of society. She wrote hymns and lives of saints and theological works. She also produced a handbook on nature, and one on medicine which combined the popular knowledge of her time with her own observations and experience. Following *Scivias* she wrote other visionary works: *The Book of Life's Merits* and *The Book of Divine Works*.

Hildegard travelled widely. She went on preaching trips during which she challenged clergy, the religious and lay people to change their ways. She died on 17 September 1179.

A feather on the breath of God

'Listen: there was once a king sitting on his throne. Around him stood great and wonderfully beautiful columns ornamented with ivory, bearing the banners of the king with great honour. Then it pleased the king to raise a small feather from the ground and he commanded it to fly. The feather flew, not because of anything in itself but because the air bore it along. Thus am I.'

Take some feathers into the session and some straws to give every child one of each.

Encourage them to play with the feathers, blowing them and making them dance. Then read the passage from Hildegard to the group. Hildegard describes her experience of God as being like a feather. Explore this image with the group. A feather has no life of its own but when it is blown it reacts and 'comes alive'. Explain that it is God who gives us life.

God's gifts

Hildegard was an exceptionally gifted woman. She used all her gifts to the glory of God. The gifts of some people are easy to recognise: a violinist, an athlete, an artist. Others are more difficult to recognise: a good listener, a willing helper, a patient friend. On a set of sticky labels list different sorts of gift: a musician, an artist, a good listener, a joker and so on. Stick one label on to the back of each child so that that child cannot see it. Take it in turns for the group to mime out the 'hidden' gift of each child until they guess what their gift is.

You could divide older children into pairs and ask them to write down what they see as their own gifts and the gifts that they see in their partner. Ask the pairs to compare each other's notes. Have they recognised the gift their friend has seen in them?

Prayer feathers

Prayer was central to Hildegard's life and to the life of a Benedictine convent. Hildegard gave daily thanks to God for the blessings he had given her. You could use the image of a feather again.

Ask each child to compose a simple prayer sentence of thanks to God for the gifts they have received from him. Ask them to write these down on strips of paper using colour felt-pens. Glue the completed prayer strips on a large sheet of paper to form a feather, drawing the central quill. Put the shorter strips at the top of the feather. Along the central quill you could write 'Thank you God'.

Fighting for Good

Michaelmas (29 September) is the feast day of St Michael and All Angels. In Jewish and Christian tradition angels are messengers and agents of God, who bring messages to human beings and intercede for them. Powerful figures, later known as archangels, appear in the book of Daniel and the apocryphal books. Some angels are named, including Michael, Raphael and Gabriel.

New Testament writers show Jesus surrounded by angels at the most important periods of his life. They announced his incarnation (Luke 1.26-38), announced his birth (Luke 2.9-15), minister to him in the desert (Matt. 4.11), strengthen him in his agony (Luke 22.43), would be ready to defend him when he is captured (Matt. 26.53) and are the first witnesses to his resurrection (Matt. 28.2-7; John 20.12ff). Jesus also refers to angels in his teaching: they are spiritual beings (Matt. 22.30) who always enjoy the vision of God in heaven (Matt. 18.10) and will accompany him at his second coming (Matt. 16.27).

'Michael' means 'who is like unto God?' In the Old Testament Michael is described as 'one of the chief princes' of the heavenly host and as a special helper of Israel (Dan. 10.13ff and 12.1). He also appears in Jude verse 9 and in the Book of Revelation. In Revelation 12.7-9 he is the principal fighter of the heavenly battle against the devil.

St Michael is often pictured slaying the dragon – as in Epstein's famous sculpture at Coventry Cathedral. His appearance in Revelation also leads to his depiction in armour and holding a sword. In medieval art he was often shown weighing souls.

Michael is also an important figure in apocryphal literature. He was seen to be a helper of Christian armies against the heathen and as a protector of individual Christians against the Devil. His cult is believed to have originated in Phrygia, where he was venerated as a healer. An apparition of St Michael on Monte Gargano in South East Italy in the late fifth century was instrumental in spreading the cult to the West. His feast day commemorates the dedication of his basilica on the Salarian Way near Rome.

2 Get the children to decorate each angel as appropriate, writing a name on each – Gabriel, Michael and Raphael. The remaining three angels can be guardian angels mentioned in the gospel reading.

3 Fix the angels wing-tip to wing-tip with double-sided sticky tape to form a collar, leaving a gap so that the children can put it round their necks.

FOR OLDER CHILDREN

A St Michael's dragon

The Revelation story can be told and then acted out with a large dragon (in most versions of the Bible the devil is portrayed here as a dragon). Here is a way children can make a dragon.

You will need assorted clean, empty cardboard boxes of different sizes, paper, paint or felt-tip pens, scissors, red crêpe paper, string, large beads or dry macaroni, glue, sticky shapes and collage materials.

1 Get the children to paint each box, or cover with paper and then colour or decorate.

2 Make a hole at both ends of each box.

3 Thread each box on to a long piece of string, with the largest box for the head and the other boxes in descending order of size. Knot the string at each side of the boxes.

4 Make the tail with beads or macaroni, and knot string firmly at each end.

5 Paint on eyes and scales.

6 Cut a mouth opening in the head and fix red crêpe paper flames to come out of the mouth.

Learning to fight the good fight

Many children confuse angels with fairies, perhaps because teaching about them usually comes at Christmas and Easter, when they get a brief mention. As angels are God's messengers, there to support us and help us fight evil, they merit the importance given to them on this festival for St Michael and All Angels. Many children will have heard the Eucharistic prayer 'therefore with angels and archangels ...' The New Testament reading for the day is the story of the War in Heaven (Rev. 12.7-12). The gospel is Matthew 18.1-6, 10, which mentions guardian angels. All these passages can be drawn on to introduce activities.

FOR YOUNGER CHILDREN

A collar of angels

There are many different kinds of angel in the Bible. This activity is to show small children some of the them.

6 cm

7 cm

You will need a piece of card, white paper, scissors, pencils, felt-tip pens or crayons, and double-sided sticky tape.

1 Make a template for an angel in card and cut out enough for each child to have six.

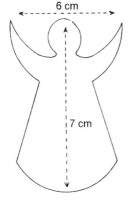

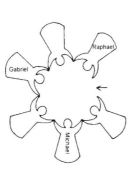

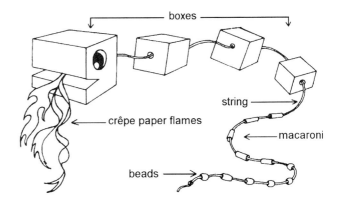

A Saint for All Ages

Few saints have inspired such affection and loyalty as St Francis. His popularity has lasted for centuries; his appeal is as lively to children and adults today as it was nearly 800 years ago.

Francis was born into a rich merchant's family in Assisi; until he was 20 he worked for his father in the family's cloth business. Francis enjoyed life, and was known in the town as gallant and high-spirited. During a long illness Francis decided to devote himself to prayer and service of the poor. On a pilgrimage to Rome he exchanged his clothes with those of a beggar, and spent the rest of the day begging. This experience had a profound effect on him and his attitude to poverty.

When he returned to Assisi, Francis devoted his time to caring for lepers and repairing the ruined church of St Damiano. One morning, while praying in the church of Portiuncula, he heard the commission of Christ to the 12 disciples. Francis understood this to be directed to him personally. He left his staff and shoes and put on a long dark garment girded with a cord and began his new mission. The simplicity of his message and call to poverty attracted many followers. Francis drew up a simple rule of life for himself and his friends.

The followers of St Francis became known as the Friars Minor. A settled rule of life for the friars was drawn up in 1221; after further revision, it was authorised by Pope Honorius III. The distinguishing mark of this rule, the Regula Bullata, was the insistence on the complete poverty not only for individual friars but also for the whole order. The friars had to live by work of their hands but were forbidden to own any property or accept money. In 1212 Francis' ideas were accepted by St Clare, a lady of Assisi who founded a similar society for women centred on the church of St Damiano. This Second Order of Franciscans became known as Poor Clares. In 1221 Francis founded the Tertiaries, a group of people who lived in the world and wanted to adopt his ideals as far as was compatible with everyday life.

Francis died on 3 October 1226. He was canonized two years later by Pope Gregory IX: his feast day is on 4 October.

have as their 'brother' or 'sister'. Ask them to explain their choice. Get them to think about what it means if something in creation is my 'brother' or 'sister': that we must love and care and be concerned for it.

Ask each child to draw, or make from material or coloured paper, their new-found 'sister' or 'brother'; then attach all this 'family' to a large sheet of card to make a collage picture of creation. The collage could carry the heading 'Praise God the Father of all creation'.

FOR OLDER CHILDREN

A way of life

St Francis chose to live in poverty. Remind the children how St Francis sold a bale of his father's best silk and gave the money to a priest to repair a ruined church. Francis's father was furious and took him to the market-place, where he ticked his son off for stealing from him when he had always given Francis whatever he wanted. Francis took off all his clothes and gave them back to his father saying, 'Here are the clothes you have given me. From now on, I will obey only my Father in Heaven.'

Discuss this story with the children; point out that Francis chose to live without fine clothes and all the things he wanted. Ask them to make a list of the things they would like for next Christmas. Then get them to cross out all those things they could live without. Is this difficult for them?

FOR YOUNGER CHILDREN

A St Francis collage

St Francis regarded the whole of God's creation as part of his family. He called the sun, 'brother sun' and the water 'sister water'. The hymn of praise composed at the end of his life, called the Canticle of the Sun can be found in most hymn books: All Creatures of Our God and King.

Invite the children to think about all the birds, animals, trees, flowers, fruits, insects, fish, etc. in God's creation and choose one they would like to

Praise God the father of all Creation

Franciscans live by a rule of life. Some of the children will be familiar with the Brownie or Cub Promise and be able to explain it. Remind them that a rule does not have to be a lot of don'ts, but a statement of what 'I intend to be'. Look at what St Francis said to his father, and the prayer of St Francis (Make me a channel of your peace), with the children. Divide the group into pairs and ask them to decide on three statements of 'What I intend to be' which they could write on a special card. Suggest that they put these cards in their bedroom and try to follow their own 'rule of life'.

The Healing Evangelist

S t Luke is believed to have been a doctor: the celebration of his festival on 18 October has often been a time when the churches remember health and healing.

According to tradition St Luke was the author of the Gospel which bears his name and of the Acts of the Apostles. Most of the information we have about this evangelist is in the New Testament. The book of Acts gives a number of clues. The 'we' sections in Acts 16, 20, 27 and 28 are believed to have formed part of Luke's travel journal. He accompanied St Paul on several of his missionary journeys. Eusebius identifies him as one of the first members of the Christian community at Antioch. From the fourth chapter of Colossians Luke is identified as a physician; it is likely he was a Gentile.

Outside the New Testament texts there are other clues about St Luke. According to later legend he was one of the 70 (Luke 10.1) sent out by Jesus to heal and preach and the unnamed disciple of Emmaus (Luke 24.13-35). The Anti-Marcionite Prologues state that St Luke was unmarried, wrote his Gospel in Greece and died at the age of 84.

In addition to being the patron saint of doctors St Luke is also patron to artists: one tradition maintains he was a painter.

Discuss with the group what the following sayings could mean:

- Two heads are better than one.
- Two's company, three's a crowd.
- Two strings to his bow.

Before the session make a list of famous couples where the skills of one have complemented the other's: Moses and Aaron, Hansel and Gretel, Robin Hood and Little John, Laurel and Hardy, Torvill and Deane, Batman and Robin and so on. On strips of paper or card write the two names on either end of the strip. Cut through the centre of the strip in a jigsaw shape so that the two names are separated and will fit together again (see diagram). Make each jigsaw-join slightly different so that the children know when they have got the right pair. Before the session hide the pieces around the room for the group to find. When they have found all the

Praying for the sick

St Luke's-tide is an appropriate time to focus on people who are ill. Discuss with the group all the people they know around them who are ill. What is wrong with them? How is their life changed by their illness? Have any of the group ever been ill? What was it like, and who looked after them? What made them feel better?

With the help of the vicar and people in the congregation find out about the people on the intercessions list. Explain to the children that Christians pray to God for sick people. It is important to explain that God's healing reaches the whole person, body, mind and spirit. Healing may include a physical cure, but it is not to be understood in this narrow sense alone. Some people remain ill and yet are healed. In our prayers we try to work within God's healing purposes.

The group can then make an intercessions book. Ask them to draw a picture of a person they know who is ill. Underneath the drawing ask them to compose a special prayer for that person. The different drawings can then be gathered together to make an intercessions book to be used by the group as part of their prayers.

The group could also make St Luke's-tide greetings cards to send to those who are

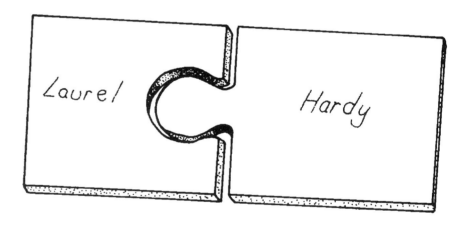

housebound or in hospital, or make a tape of songs to cheer them up.

Famous pairs

When the 70 are sent out to heal and preach by Jesus in Luke 10 (and Luke 9.1-6), they go out in pairs. Discuss with the group the advantages of sending disciples out in pairs rather than individually. Luke himself was a companion for Paul on his missionary journeys. Sometimes two people working together can be more effective than one. They might have different skills or a different way of seeing something.

pairs you can discuss how the different skills of the pairs complemented each other.

Ask the group to pretend that they are one of the 70 sent out by Jesus to heal and preach. Who would they choose to go with them, and why? What skills and special gifts has their friend got? How would they tell people about Jesus?

Crown Them with Many Crowns

A ll Saints' tide provides an opportunity for celebrating the lives of all of those, living and dead, who have dedicated their lives to God. The season also provides an excellent opportunity for a great church party and celebration. These activity suggestions take the theme of crowns and the Christian path of life. They can be incorporated into a family service, Sunday school or a party.

'Blessed is the man who endures trial, for when he has stood the test he will receive the crown of life which God has promised to those who love him' (James 1.12, RSV). Discuss this verse with the group.

- What do they think is meant by the 'crown of life'?
- When are crowns used?
- Apart from the crowns of kings, where else do crowns appear in the New Testament?

For most children crowns are associated with kings, queens or perhaps pub signs and Burger King restaurants. In the passage from James the crown is seen as a sign of victory. In the New Testament there are two Greek words used for 'crown': 'diadema' – diadem, the mark of royalty which is found in Rev. 12.3, 13.1, 19.12; and 'stephanos' – wreath, which is a garland type of crown. This wreath, garland or corona (Latin) was the garland given as a prize to those who were victors in the games: see 1 Cor. 9.25, 2 Tim. 2.5. It is also the word used of Jesus's crown of thorns.

The image of the wreath crown in the New Testament is a rich one to explore with children: a crown of righteousness (2 Tim. 4.8); a crown of glory (1 Peter 5.4); a crown of life (Rev. 2.10). In Christian art the saints are often depicted wearing crowns or holding a wreath of martyrdom. Like kings and queens, the saints are the elect, the specially chosen ones. Like athletes, they have been victorious in their task. Discuss with the older members of the group how the Christian life is like that of an athlete – the sense of purpose and goal, the need for constant training and practice.

Christian journey and the choices they have had to make along the way.

The scroll can be a series of pictures, or text and pictures.

These scrolls could be displayed at All Saints' tide around the church.

FOR THE WHOLE GROUP

An All Saints' T-shirt

For a special celebration or party the group could design their own T-shirts. Ask the children to find out about a particular local saint, or the saint of dedication, or someone they think of as a saint who is alive today. They can then find out the emblem of that saint or design one for themselves. The week before the activity ask the children to bring in an old plain washed T-shirt and an overall to protect themselves.

The Early Learning Centre and other toy and craft shops now sell fabric-paint felt pens. The teacher will also need to provide adequate newspaper covering to protect tables and floors, card to fit inside each T-shirt so that the design does not seep through more than one layer, enough drawing materials, and paper and an iron and ironing board. There will also need to be extra adult help.

On a sheet of paper the same size as the front of their T-shirt the children should draw the emblem for their saint, with a wreath above it. Once the children are confident of their design they can then draw it in fabric

FOR YOUNGER CHILDREN

A wreath crown

Using the laurel template given, produce enough laurel leaves from card for the children to make their own crowns. The group can then colour their leaves and decorate them. To make the crown, staple enough of the leaves together to fit around the child's head. The group might like to dress up as different saints and process into church on All Saints' Day wearing their wreaths.

FOR OLDER CHILDREN

A path of life

The Christian way or path of life involves making choices for good. Like an athlete at the Olympics, the Christian has a goal.

Older children can draw their own path of life on a long scroll of paper. They can plot their journey from birth until now, marking on the paper the people and things which have helped them on their

pens on the T-shirt itself. It is important that they follow the fabric pen manufacturer's instructions on how to use the pens or paints.

The Many-Sided St Martin

Concern for the work of the church in rural areas began centuries before ACORA (The Archbishops' Commission on Rural Areas). The extraordinary vision of St Martin in fifth-century France helped the Church to move out from its city habitat and into the countryside.

St Martin was a man of many talents and careers. He is the patron saint of soldiers, horses and their riders, beggars, geese, winegrowers and innkeepers. Historically he was influential in the monastic movement and in setting up a rudimentary parochial system.

St Martin was born in either 316 or 335 in Pannonia (Hungary), and followed in his father's footsteps by becoming an officer in the Roman army. Unlike his father he became a Christian.

The legend associated with his baptism is that when he was stationed at Amiens (France) in winter he met a beggar begging for alms. St Martin felt sorry for him and divided his cloak in two giving half to the beggar. That night in a dream Christ appeared to him and said 'Martin, yet a catechumen (a Christian under instruction), has covered me with this garment.' St Martin was baptised and became convinced that his Christian faith prevented him from being a soldier. He appeared before the Roman emperor, who accused Martin of cowardice and put him in prison.

Years later Martin became a disciple of Hilary of Poitiers. The new disciple wanted to be a hermit and Hilary gave him land at Ligugé. Here he was joined by other hermits. Traditionally this was the first monastery in Gaul. Martin continued to live as a monk when he became Bishop of Tours in 372. He lived in a cell two miles from the city: disciples gathered around him, living in huts and caverns.

This community formed the nucleus of the famous monastery of Marmoutier. Martin's asceticism was not popular with his fellow bishops, who saw the saint's poverty as undignified. The saint went on to found other monasteries in Gaul and from these he extended his work of mission into rural areas. The other famous legends belong to this era when Martin was attributed with destroying heathen temples and sacred trees. He became known as a miracle worker and healer.

St Martin died on 8 November 397, and was buried in Tours on 11 November. A life written by his friend Sulpicius Severus increased the popularity of his cult. In Britain his feast day (11 November) coincided with the season for hiring servants and for killing cattle. The expression 'a St Martin's summer' refers to the fine weather that often appears at that time of year.

These activity suggestions focus on the different functions St Martin took on in his life, and explore the French connection.

Acting out the story

Tell the story of St Martin to the group. Encourage the younger children to make props which illustrate the different stages of St Martin's life: a soldier's sword, a divided cloak, a monk's scapular, a mitre, a bare branch adorned with paper leaves and flowers (for a St Martin's summer). Most of these props can be made from paper. The group can then act out different scenes from St Martin's life.

Older children can also act out the story after they have scripted or discussed their own production of it. Alternatively they might enjoy doing a fifth-century 'This is your Life'.

Making a story book

Older children can write their own illustrated story book of St Martin's life for the younger children.

The French connection

Get the group to find out the appropriate French words for Martin's different roles in life and the particular qualities he needed to fulfil them.

The group can then make a large chain of paper people. They can dress up each St Martin in the appropriate outfit labelling each figure, soldat, moine, évêque, etc. Where the arms interlock they can find a 'link word' which describes the qualities St Martin needed to fulfil both roles, e.g. he needed humility to be both a bishop and a monk (see illustration). The completed paper chain can serve as a reminder of the different vocations Christians can have.

évêque   humilité   moine   générosité   soldat

A Saintly Queen

ST MARGARET OF SCOTLAND

16 NOVEMBER

St Margaret of Scotland was a formidable woman. She was the granddaughter of two kings, mother of three kings and a queen, a religious reformer, queen of Scotland and a saint. Her biographer and chaplain Turgot also tells us she was humble, sensitive, godly and easily moved to tears.

St Margaret was born around 1046 in Hungary. Her father was Edward the Atheling, son of Edmund Ironside, the English king. Edward was in exile in King Stephen's court and there he married Agatha, a Hungarian princess. Margaret's family returned to England, but after the Norman Conquest fled to Scotland and found refuge in the court of Malcolm III. Margaret had intended to become a nun; but Malcolm was so charmed by her that he asked the young princess to marry him and become his queen.

The Scottish court of the time was not renowned for its sophistication. Turgot's life shows how Margaret's intelligence, education, sense of beauty and religious practice soon had a great influence. Malcolm feared to offend his queen: 'What she refused he refused, and what she loved, he loved for the love of her'.

Margaret was also instrumental in changing the Scottish Church. Under the guidance of Lanfranc, the Archbishop of Canterbury, she helped alter many of the existing Celtic practices to Roman ones. She was responsible for bringing in new disciplines including the regulation of the Lenten fast, Easter communion and abstinence from certain kinds of work on Sundays. She also founded many monasteries, churches and hostels for pilgrims. The abbey at Iona was revived and Dunfermline Abbey was built to be the Westminster Abbey of Scotland and a place of burial for Scottish kings.

Margaret had eight children. Three sons became kings of Scotland. Through her daughter Matilda, who married Henry I of England, the royal family of today can trace their descent from the pre-Conquest kings of England. Margaret died at the age of 47 and was buried beside Malcolm at Dunfermline.

For teachers interested in reading more about St Margaret, Floris Books have recently brought out a version of Turgot's life edited by Iain Macdonald (*St Margaret*, 0-86315-165-5).

FOR YOUNGER CHILDREN
Pearls

'She was called Margaret, that is, "a Pearl," and in the sight of God she was esteemed a lovely pearl by reason of her faith and good works' (Turgot).

The image of a pearl is a rich one to explore with children. In Matthew's Gospel (Matt. 13.45-46) the kingdom of heaven is likened to the pearl of great price.

St Margaret's name was an appropriate one ('margaron' is the Greek for pearl). She was good and beautiful and her life was devoted to God's service.

If possible take an oyster shell and a string of pearls to show to the group. Explain how pearls are formed.

Discuss with the group what it is they treasure most? What do they hold in high value, like a pearl or precious gem?

Make paper oyster shell pairs for all the children. Use the fold of the paper as the shell hinge so that the shell can be opened and closed. Then give each child a small white disc or 'pearl' to put into their shell (see diagram).

Children can draw on the pearl the thing that they most treasure. On the inside of the shell they can write a short prayer to thank God for their treasure.

FOR OLDER CHILDREN
Thread of life

Tell the story of Margaret's life to the group. Ask the children which episodes they enjoy the most and why. They could act out their favourite scenes.

Then ask each child to concentrate on one part of Margaret's life: her childhood, her return to England, her arrival by sea in Scotland, etc. All of them should then draw a picture in the centre of a white paper plate which illustrates the event they have chosen. The plates or pearls can then be mounted as a frieze, and interlinked with a thread of string to make a string of pearls to retell the story of Margaret.

A refugee

Marg'ret wore Scotland's crown
to show God's royal care;
an exiled child, her heart had known
the pain that strangers bear.
So from her castle door
no orphan turned unfed;
she touched the sick and clothed the poor,
accepted in Christ's stead.

The present Bishop of St Andrews, the Rt Revd Michael Hare Duke, wrote a special hymn for a 900th anniversary service for St Margaret in 1993. The second verse of the hymn, which is reprinted here, can be sung (to the tune Diademata, which is usually used for *Crown him with many crowns*) by the group as a reminder of Queen Margaret's good works. The full text of the hymn is printed in *Hearing the Stranger*, Cairns Publications, 1994. In preparation for Advent, groups might want to consider how they can show God's care to the exiles, orphans, sick and poor people today. With older children it might be a suitable occasion to focus on refugees and migrants.

A Ministry of Encouragement

St Hilda is one of a group of formidable women saints from Anglo-Saxon England. Her name, Hilda or Hild, means battle. Of royal blood, Hilda was a woman of strength and character who ruled the famous double monastery at Whitby with authority and wisdom.

We read about Hilda in Bede's *A History of the English Church and People*. Hilda was born in 614 and was the great-niece of King Edwin, one of the most powerful of the Northumbrian kings. In 627 she was baptised with the royal household by Paulinus, Bishop of York. Bede records that she spent 33 years in secular occupations and then spent the remainder of her life in a monastery. St Aidan gave her land on the north bank of the River Wear to set up a monastery.

She became Abbess of Hartlepool and then of 'Calcaria', possibly Tadcaster. After some years she moved to Streonshalh, later renamed Whitby by the Danes. There she became abbess of a community of monks and nuns for the remaining 23 years of her life.

Whitby became a centre of learning and spiritual leadership. Kings and queens came to Hilda for advice. Priests were trained there and Bede tells us that more than five men went on to become bishops. Although the Abbey was famous for its libraries and academic learning one of its most famous monks was Caedmon, a cowherd.

Caedmon was embarrassed because he could not sing. When his fellow workers met in the evening to sing and entertain each other Caedmon used to creep away and hide in the cowshed. One night he dreamt that a messenger of God told him to sing. In his dream Caedmon composed and sang a great poem in praise of God's creation. When he awoke Caedmon remembered the song and sang it. Hilda then encouraged him to make up more poems, and asked him to stay at the monastery as a lay brother. Caedmon composed many poems and songs in the vernacular; he became the first Anglo-Saxon popular religious poet.

The Synod of Whitby in 664 met while Hilda was abbess. At that time Northern Christianity had developed from two distinct sources, the teaching of the missionaries from Rome and the Celtic monastic traditions. The Synod of Whitby met to resolve the question of the dating of Easter as the Celtic and Roman dating were different. Hilda supported the Celtic dating but accepted the final decision of the Synod in favour of Rome. According to Bede, Hilda died at the age of 66 on 17 November 680.

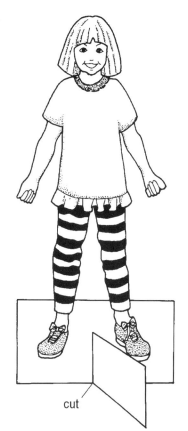

cut

Put the photograph of your church in one corner of the large sheet and the picture of the place of pilgrimage in the diagonally opposite corner. Draw a winding road connecting the two. Divide it into sections. With the group, think of encouragements and obstacles that pilgrims might face on their journey. These can be drawn or written in on the sections of the game. On the encouragement sections the player can be told to move on a number of places, and on the obstacles he can be sent back a turn or a number of places. Each child can make their own pilgrim figure from card with a card plinth attached, so that they can stand it up on the board (see drawing). The details and rules of the game can be devised by the teacher or group. But essentially it is a snakes-and-ladders game where each child throws a dice in turn and then moves their pilgrim accordingly.

FOR OLDER CHILDREN

The Caedmon connection: praise posters

Tell the story of St Hilda and Caedmon. Discuss with the children how we receive gifts from God and how Caedmon received his gift of singing, encouraged by St Hilda.

Ask each child to think of their favourite hymn or psalm. Then ask them to say why they like it. They can each write up and illustrate their choice on a large sheet of card to make a praise poster. The group can then each sing a song or a selection of songs to each other, using the praise posters as a visual aid.

A parish pilgrimage

In the early church, abbeys were important places for pilgrimage and hospitality. People would travel great distances to visit and pray at the shrines. Whitby became a popular place of pilgrimage because of St Hilda.

St Hilda's day might provide an opportunity for the congregation to organise an parish pilgrimage. This could be to a well-known pilgrimage centre in the area or to a ruined abbey or monastery. Encourage the group to find out as much as possible about the place,

its history, architecture, the people connected with it and its influence in the area. The group can then plan a pilgrimage day with suitable all-age activities that include games and worship.

FOR YOUNGER CHILDREN

A pilgrimage game

You will need large sheets of paper, card, drawing materials, scissors, glue, photographs of your home church and place of pilgrimage.

A Bishop Who Challenged Kings

'If you require a monument, look around you.' Sir Christopher Wren's famous epitaph applies equally to St Hugh, who is perhaps best remembered as the builder of Lincoln Cathedral. Yet Lincoln was but one of many achievements in a lively ministry.

Hugh was born around 1135 into a noble family in Avalon, near Grenoble, and joined the Carthusian order at the age of 15. He was content to enter the life of the cloister, and it was with reluctance that he travelled across the Channel to take charge of the first Carthusian house to be founded in England.

When he arrived at Witham in Somerset he found decaying buildings and a demoralised group of monks. He immediately set about reform, and within six years he had restored both the buildings and the monastic ideal, winning the trust of locals and of the king at the same time. The biography of Hugh by Adam, his chaplain, tells us that Henry II 'moved by the fame of his holiness, prevailed upon him to come to England and afterwards, with the consent of the canons, made him Bishop of Lincoln. But the man of God recoiled from such election, and would not take the see until he had been elected again, and that time freely.' In those days the diocese of Lincoln covered most of central England from the Humber to the Thames.

As Bishop of Lincoln, Hugh was never afraid to stand up to the monarch and others in authority. On one famous occasion Hugh was in dispute with King Richard over the King's right to levy a tax to fund an army. Hugh refused to pay. Richard ordered the seizure of Hugh's income. But the royal servants, out of reverence for Hugh but also in fear of excommunication, dragged their feet. The result was a stalemate which was eventually broken by Hugh's initiative.

He went to France to confront the king face to face. He arrived at Richard's new castle on the Seine during mass. He went straight up to the king who sat on his royal throne, flanked by bishops, and greeted him. When Richard refused to repay the compliment, Hugh grabbed his tunic and shook him, demanding the proper courtesy. Very unwillingly, Richard greeted him. Later, during the peace, Richard walked over to Hugh and gave him the kiss of peace. After the service the two men met and Hugh won the day.

Hugh's fame also rests on his defence of the poor, lepers and outcasts and on his protection of Jews against persecution and hostility. He was also, legend has it, cast somewhat in the St Francis mould. He had a pet swan – some say it was a goose – who pined for him while he was on his many travels, and who perked up when he returned home.

Hugh died in London in 1200 aged about 65. Adam writes 'All the nobility of England attended his funeral at Lincoln, and the kings of England and Scotland.' Many miracles were claimed both during and after the funeral, and he was formally canonized in 1220.

The King

St Hugh

Swan

Leper

Peasant

FOR OLDER CHILDREN

A modern St Hugh

Tell the story of St Hugh to the children especially the incident with King Richard. Ask them if they know any modern bishops who have spoken out against secular authority in God's name when they have seen something that is wrong or unjust. What have been the consequences of their actions? The names might include Archbishop Janani Luwum, Archbishop Trevor Huddleston, Archbishop Oscar Romero and Archbishop Desmond Tutu.

Ask the children to tell the story of their chosen leader in words and pictures in a scrapbook.

FOR YOUNGER CHILDREN

A St Hugh card game

The aim of this card game is to help the children understand that St Hugh had charity for all people. In his eyes each one of God's people was of value whether a leper, a peasant or a king.

You will need a copy of the template of the people for each child, three copies of the swan template for each group of four children, colouring materials, scissors, glue and card. Cut copies of the template into individual pictures. Glue these on to larger pieces of card to form playing cards. Ask the children to colour in their set of characters.

The purpose of the game is for each child to collect their own set of cards. Divide the children into groups of four. To play the game, collect the cards from the children and shuffle with the three uncoloured swan cards. Place the pack face down in the centre of the group. Deal four cards to each child. The children decide which cards they need to discard. In turn the children place a card they do not want at the bottom of the pack and pick up a new card from the top. The game is played until one child has their own set of cards.

This game can be modified in a number of ways. Very young children might prefer to play snap with the pack.

Make Your Own Music

Cecilia is one of those saints whose fame extends far beyond the Church and whose memory is widely treasured. She probably lived in the second or third century and was buried in Rome. Little more than this is actually known about her. Although many churches and music groups will celebrate her feast day on 22 November, St Cecilia is not in the ASB Calendar.

Her great popularity is largely due to a late fifth-century legend. It records that she was a young Christian patrician, betrothed to a pagan called Valerian. As she had already vowed her virginity to God she refused to consummate the marriage. Both her husband and his brother, Tiburtius, became Christians and were martyred; and Cecilia trod the same path. A version of the story says 'As the organs (at her wedding feast) were playing, Cecilia sang (in her heart) to the Lord, saying: may my heart remain unsullied, so that I be not confounded.' That seems to be the origin of her patronage of music.

1.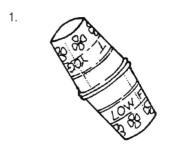

2.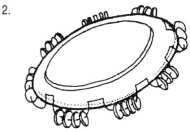

St Cecilia's Day provides an occasion for a celebration of music in church or in a children's class. These activity suggestions are designed so that children can make their own musical instruments. Apart from the wooden xylophone all the instruments use everyday objects and can be made fairly quickly with adult supervision.

Percussion instruments

Effective **shakers** can be made from many household objects. Rice, dried beans (not kidney beans), marbles, buttons, lentils and macaroni can be used to provide the inside of shakers. The shaker can be made from taping together two empty yogurt pots as shown in figure 1.

A **tambourine** can be made by threading bottle tops in groups of three or four and attaching them loosely to a paper plate (figure 2).

Castanets can be made from a piece of card and two 10-pence coins. On a strip of card score straight line down the centre. Reverse the card and score two lines, 1cm either side of the centre. On the original side score a further two lines 2cm from the centre line. Concertina the card as shown in figure 4. Secure the back of the folded card with tape so that the flaps spring apart. Using Blu-tak, fix 10-pence pieces facing each other inside the flaps. They must be directly opposite each other. The children might then like to cut out the flaps in a traditional castanet shape.

Pitch instruments

For those teachers with a bit of extra time an effective **xylophone** can be made from different lengths of dowelling. Tie string around each length of dowelling as shown in figure 3, tying a knot at the top and bottom of each length so that the dowelling does not slip down the string. A better musical sound is obtained if a hole is drilled (by an adult) at either end of the dowelling for the string to be threaded through. This can be played with a wooden spoon or beater.

A simple **water xylophone** can be made by filling milk bottles with different measures of water. The smaller the air space left the higher the note. This can be played with a stick. It can also be a wind instrument and children can experiment by blowing across the top of the bottle like a flute.

An **elastic-band guitar** can be made from elastic bands of different sizes and thicknesses around an open shoe box, or open biscuit tin (figure 5).

Children themselves will know of many ways of making music, from the comb-and-tissue paper harmonica to the saucepan-lid cymbals. If your church has a pipe organ, ask the organist to show the children how the different pipes work.

Once made, the instruments can be used to accompany a favourite song or hymn. The song *Father, we want to thank you*, written by Susan Sayers and arranged by Frances M Kelly, in *Many Ways to Praise* (Palm Tree Press), is a good song to start with. Alternatively, teachers might like to look at

3.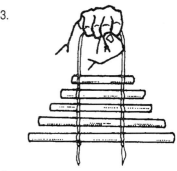

4.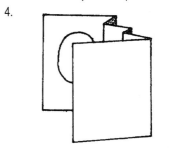

5.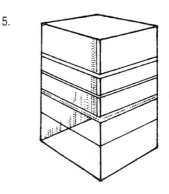

Psalm 150 with the children. This great hymn of praise mentions many musical instruments, and the children could shout out each verse, using the most appropriate instrument.

The Patron Saint of Scotland

O f St Andrew, one of the 12 apostles, we know from the New Testament that he was Simon Peter's brother (Mark 1.16-20); a native of Bethsaida (John 1.44) who lived in Capernaum. He was a fisherman (Matt. 4.18-20) who had been a follower of John the Baptist before he followed Jesus (John 1.35-40). In Mark 13.3 Andrew is linked to the inner circle of disciples. Special mention is made of him in the miracle of the feeding of the multitude, where he finds the boy with the five loaves of bread and two fish (John 6.8ff), and in the episode of the Greeks who wished to meet Jesus (John 12.20-22).

Legends surround his later life. One links him with Patras in Greece, another with Constantinople. Since about 750 he has been the patron saint of Scotland.

The legend linking St Andrew with Scotland is that St Rule, a native of Patras in the fourth century, was told by an angel to take the relics of St Andrew to an unknown destination. The saint travelled until the angel told him to stop in Fife, where he built a church to house the relics. The town later became known as St Andrews.

One legend says Andrew was crucified at Patras. The apostle acknowledged that he was not worthy to die as Jesus had died and so elected to be crucified on a Greek X-shaped (saltire) cross. This cross became his symbol. In the Scottish flag it appears as a white cross (for St Andrew's purity) on a blue background (representing the sea), which also forms part of the Union Jack. His other symbol is a fishing-net, reflecting his patronage of fishermen and sailors.

The Feast of St Andrew has been celebrated since the sixth century on 30 November. In the Anglican Communion, St Andrewstide is often observed as a time of special prayer for the Church's mission.

Activities for St Andrewstide could focus on St Andrew the disciple and missionary, and could explore modern methods of evangelism.

FOR YOUNGER CHILDREN

Footprint frieze

Younger children could play a follow-the-leader game and make a footprint frieze. For the game, the children form a circle. The leader does a repetitive action which the children can follow, clapping, skipping, etc. The leader then selects a new leader who chooses a new action for the children to follow. Use this game to lead in to the story of St Andrew.

Before the session, write 'We are following Jesus' on the top of a large sheet of paper. In the class, let the children draw around each other's feet on A4 sheets of paper and cut the shapes out. Include any adults present. Get the older children to write their names on their own shapes and stick them on to the sheet to form a frieze. Talk with the children about the way the sign of the cross is used in baptism to mark the followers of Jesus. Then add a cross at the front of the line of footsteps.

FOR OLDER CHILDREN

A Good News poster

Older children can make a 'Spread the Good News' poster.

Talk with them about St Andrew as a missionary, 'a fisher of men', and use this to lead into an exploration of the Decade of Evangelism. Explore what ideas the children have about this. Discuss how methods of evangelism have changed since St Andrew's time. The children can now take part in making a good-news poster which helps them discover modern ways of evangelism.

Get them to draw or cut out pictures from magazines which show today's methods and tools of evangelism. These might include pictures of preaching, drama, music, clowning, television, video, books, radio, Bibles, etc. Ask one child to draw, colour and cut a large St Andrew shield, adding the words 'spread the good news' on white labels in the four segments of the shield. Stick the shield in the centre of a large sheet of paper. Get the children to add their pictures round the shield; link each picture to the shield with lengths of wool.

Other books for church children's groups published by

NATIONAL SOCIETY/ CHURCH HOUSE PUBLISHING

Seasons, Saints and Sticky Tape
Ideas and activities for celebrating Christian festivals
Nicola Currie and Jean Thomson

A practical, well-illustrated resource book for church children's groups, primary schools and families, full of tried-and-tested ideas for making Christian festivals fun for children.

£7.95

Step This Way 1 and 2
A course for 5-7s in Church
Edited by Marjorie Freeman

A whole year's course to use with 5-7-year-olds in your church. Includes vivid stories especially written for this age group and attractive, photocopiable TAKE IT HOME sheets.

£5.95 each

Be a Church Detective
A young person's guide to old churches
Clive Fewins

An entertaining introduction to the mysterious secrets of crypts, vaults, graveyards and towers for 8-14-year-olds. Packed full of historical information, fact boxes, drawings and cartoons to encourage the junior 'church crawler'.
Over 4,000 copies already in print.

£4.95

THE NATIONAL SOCIETY
A Christian Voice in Education

The National Society (Church of England) for Promoting Religious Education is a charity which supports all those involved in Christian education – teachers and school governors, students and parents, clergy and lay people – with the resources of its RE Centres, archives, courses, conferences and publications.

Founded in 1811, the Society was chiefly responsible for setting up the nationwide network of Church schools in England and Wales and still provides grants for building projects and legal and administrative advice for headteachers and governors. It now publishes a wide range of books, pamphlets and audio-visual items, and two magazines, *Crosscurrent* and *Together*.

For further details of the Society or a copy of our current catalogue, please contact:

The Promotions Secretary,
The National Society,
Church House,
Great Smith Street,
London
SW1P 3NZ
Telephone: 071-222 1672